My Silent Partner

Ben A. Savelli

Ben A. Savelli
Publisher

MY SILENT PARTNER

First Edition
Copyright © 1996 by
Ben A. Savelli

Library of Congress Catalog Card Number: 96-92542

ISBN 0-7880-0906-0   PRINTED IN U.S.A.

Dedication

For a long time, I wondered what made me happy. Was it money? No. Was it fame? No. Was it work? What was it? I had to go back to what really made me tick. The only way I could find out was to go back to the one clue I had. It was my mother. And let me tell you why.

My mother only was happy when everyone else was happy. She was a 100% giver. In her prime, she gave and gave and gave. She had power with our grocery store and the food she controlled. She cooked and cooked and found joy in giving. Now giving is one thing, but giving with never a thought of return is almost a quality not found among us mortals.

We grew up with a 99% give ratio and a 1% take formula. We were forced to receive at times, but our mother was only happy when she was giving. I am dedicating this book to her. She never gave to receive. Her biggest and best way to show how happy it made her, was her cooking. She was master of that.

To you, Mom, the champion giver, I dedicate this book. The secret of giving is to give without wanting something in return; to be pure… Mom, you were 100% pure!!!

Acknowledgements

For untiring assistance in the direct writing of "My Silent Partner," my heart goes out to my daughter, Marilyn Cornejo. Also, for her never-ending patience, special thanks to my sister Roberta Hayderi, and for computer expertise and editing, my niece Sandy Halpin. To my son, Gary Savelli, I owe thousands of hours of advice, technical work, and suggestions.

For the factual information relative to Galileo High School and the Galileo High School Hall of Fame, the entire effort belongs to Jack McCaffrey. He and former principal James Kearney brought to life the great program which brought such athletic fame to San Francisco.

To my best "pal" and life-time friend, Walter Biondi, I owe just about everything. Walt ought to receive the "medal of honor" for the many hours he devoted to me and my book. "Ditto" goes to my co-best pal, William P. Brachna, alias just plain "Bill".

Finally we come to the crew at the office of Basic West Insurance Agency, who always made me feel as if I had never left the firm to write this book. My son Gary, who works there, practically re-wrote the entire script. Tina Treichler, my daughter Janet Bonilla, Dolly Vella, and Roberta Hayderi listened to me on almost every office break, as I reviewed and re-reviewed my stories. Thanks to all of them for the love, time, money, photocopies, phone calls, and everything else I needed to finish this product.

And most of all, thanks to the man who made this story possible: "My Silent Partner."

About The Author

The author of "My Silent Partner," Ben A. Savelli, received his preliminary writing experience as sports editor of the Galileo High School paper in 1936-1937.

Ben enrolled in a school known for its excellence in journalism, College of the Pacific, at Stockton, California. After a great first year, Ben was elected to the publications committee, a position reserved for seniors only , but World War II ruined his writing ambitions. He was transferred to the University Of California at Berkeley to finish his education. As Ben's brother had already been drafted, Ben was allowed to continue his education until graduation in 1941.

After World War II, Ben continued his writing career, editing a neighborhood paper for 27 years. He was president of Basic West Insurance and retired after an insurance career of over 50 years.

As his writing career continued, over 50 articles appeared in major insurance magazines. Today, Ben has now retired from the insurance business and is devoting 100% of his time to his writing career.

Mr. Savelli is working on his second book, soon to be published, entitled "The Magic Of Giving." It will be published in 1997. His third book also is expected to be completed by 1997. This will be the author's favorite book, "I Went Broke In The Boom."

Ben is married and lives with his wife, Evelyn, in San Francisco, California. They have four children: Marilyn, Robert, Gary, and Janet.

Table Of Contents

1.	The Store	11
2.	The Swimming Suit	18
3.	Mary, Mary Can't Compare-y	20
4.	Nana	27
5.	Tata the Big Patata	34
6.	Berkeley Bobby	39
7.	Monday Night	46
8.	The Game Before the Game	51
9.	Gamblers Unanimous	57
10.	Take Me Out to the Old Brawl Game	64
11.	Growing Up	69
12.	The Zoot Suit	74
13.	One Polk and Two Fell…	77
14.	Ben Discovers Galileo	82
15.	Freddy's Famous Sandwiches	89
16.	Upstairs in the "A"	93
17.	The Song Sheets	97
18.	Richie's 17 Months Older than I Am	100
19.	What's Right is Write	109
20.	The Water Boy	114
21.	Follies Night at College of Pacific	118
22.	College Daze	124
22 & 1/2.	The War and Treasure Island Didn't Mix	127
23.	Patriotism	131

24. First Alert–The War Starts with a
    Bang for Ben   134
25. The Case of the Missing K.P.   141
26. Army Specialized Training Program   148
27. Sister Roberta   158
28. V-E Day, or Halfway Home   164
29. B.V.D. Underaware   171
30. I Remember It Well   178
31. Let's Play Dominoes   182
32. My Most Embarrassing Moment   188
33. Ike Could Have Been a Contender–Patton
    Pays Ben a Visit   193
34. Some Sunday Morning   199
35. Whatta You Gonna Do When the
    War is Over?   203
36. Born on the Fourth of July   210
37. The Bridges of San Fran   215
38. The Birthday Bomb: August 9th   220
39. See Us Freeze   224
40. The End of the Beginning   228
41. The Last Hurrah   234

Preface

Four weeks ago, I had four wires attached to my brain and there was little hope for me. I asked the Good Lord if he could help me... I would be his SILENT PARTNER for the rest of my life. I have always wanted to WRITE. He must have accepted my offer because I am still here... Now my SILENT PARTNER and I will proceed with the business at hand. We are naming our first book in His honor.

MY SILENT PARTNER
By Ben A. Savelli

This was where it all started. My father was a tailor. Business was sew-sew, so he left and became a grocer.

Chapter 1

The Store

Over sixty years ago, my parents bought a grocery store in San Francisco. **My dad had tried being a tailor but business was only sew-sew, so he sold his tailor shop and opened an Italian deli.** He would feature mostly deli items and fruits and vegetables. My dad wanted us to be open from 6:00 a.m. to 10:00 p.m. As the chain store across the street was only open from 8:00 a.m. to 7:00 p.m., we would have an extra five hours to sell with no competition in sight.

We proceeded to make some wooden fixtures for the produce on one side of the store and on the other side, **we had an ice box or, as my father used to say in "Itralian," the Ice-A-Box** ... There was no refrigeration in those days like you see today. We made some shelves against the walls for canned goods and a few counters. That was it. **You could have bought the entire store, including us kids, for about two hundred dollars** ...

Our prices were so low they could see bottom ... carrots, beets, and turnips, 3 bunches for 10 cents; potatoes, 10 pounds for 25 cents; bananas, 20 cents per dozen; strawberries, 3 baskets for a quarter. On the other side of the store, the deli stuff was low also: 30 cents a pound for baloney; 40 cents for cheese; 60 cents for ham; and 80 cents for prosciutto (Italian ham), which now runs $22.00 per pound ... now you get a picture of what it was like in a depression!

Our very first customer was a lady that lived in the alley behind the store ... her place was three stories up and my brother Rich or I had to bring her order up and leave it at the door; then she would pay for it at the end of the week. She only bought a small table cream, which cost 21 cents. (I always said, **you can't beat table cream!**) We had to do anything to start our business! My father would make us walk up to ten blocks or more for as little as a $1.00 purchase ... on long walks we had a little metal wagon and we used that. Well, we were in business!

My brother was very good with figures, so he stayed at the cash register. Our register could only print one price at a time ... if you bought seven items, we could only ring up the total. My father used to add everything up in his head as he pointed to each item: .20, .42, .59, 1.08, 1.27, 1.42, 1.67. My idea was to write down the individual amounts on a paper item and then add them up. For example, if the customer had bought some salami, cheese, or other cold cuts, which he usually did, I would just total everything up on the white paper we used to wrap those items in. Little did I know I was ahead of my time; today's markets itemize, add, subtract, multiply, divide, and conquer ... still, it was tough just ringing up one figure.

Soon all of us knew we had a winner — "we" meaning my sister Roberta; me; my brother, Rich; our mother, Mary; and our father, Robert or Bob. That was it. Actually, my sister Roberta, or Bert, was not born yet, but I thought I would mention her because Bert always will be claiming we left her out of the story!

We ate our meals in the back room of the store and a lot of the customers would buy something and then make an excuse to say hello to my mother and walk in the back, where the kitchen was ... we had many people tasting my mother's cooking, but it was good for business, as it became a family affair.

My mother was like her name, Mary ... she was pure ... she would give her heart for anyone. Our Mary was a genius when it came to cooking ... scallopini, lasagne, meat balls and spaghetti, pasta of all kinds ... every night something different and more and more customers got on a first name basis with Bob and Mary. Before I forget it, I want to tell you about the old Italian cooking ... we had all kinds of olive oil ... my mother used to use up one gallon, at least, per week ... At 12 years of age, what did I know about fats or cholesterol!?!? ... The food was out of this world!

I used to worry more about my mother than my father ... why is it always that way? When there were boxes to be moved or other heavy work, I would always try to do it, so my mother wouldn't have to be involved.

My dad was great at what he did best. He used to sing opera with some really rich customers and it would attract a lot of fun people. Some opera singers now living on Russian Hill loved my father ... **they would sing their hearts out for a little Italian food, so at our age we heard many an aria.** My father was so proud and would always join in on the Italian ones. Somehow my dad could handle higher-class situations better than the rest of us.

On the other hand, my father's selection of credit customers was not that great. He trusted everyone and it led to a lot of bad debts. Many people owed us $30.00, which was about a month's supply of groceries. In those days, that was a lot of money; nowadays, it is a drop in the bucket ... but I am only telling you how it was in those days.

My father used to tell me not to talk about myself, but to find out about the customer and the next time talk about what he told me ... for example, if he mentions he plays a lot of golf, next time bring up something you think he might like to hear such as, **"A golf ball is a golf ball, no matter how you putt it."** Soon I became the top salesman of the store ... **too bad nobody buys tops anymore!**

I remember one older lady who evidently had an injury or a stroke so she always had her cane. She would point the cane at the strawberries and say, "Too bad they are not real firm," or at the cauliflower and say, "They look all brown." My mother, brother, and father would not like waiting on her ... Her name was Mrs. Sargent and she sounded like a sergeant, too! So I took it upon myself, as I was the smallest in the store, to wait on her ... and I did. Being 12 or 13 years old, I had an energy that I wish I had today ... **today, the only energy around here is in a battery, and they are always wearing out!** But let's get back to this story that you aren't even interested in anyway.

When Mrs. Sargent came in the next day I said, "Hello, Mrs. Sargent. I'm Benny and I would like to wait on you. I know you like strawberries, so when my father brought the crates in, I picked the two best baskets for you, and they are real firm and sweet, too.

I tasted one from another basket and I said to myself, 'If you don't like these strawberries, nobody will!' ... and then I know you always like melons and my father got a real bargain on cantaloupes ... And look! I made a new sign for our melon section — it says, '**O Honey Dew, we Cantaloupe.**'" After that **Mrs. Sargent and I were on a first-name basis — I called her Mrs. Sargent and she called me Benny.**

From then until the time I grew up and went off to college, I waited on Mrs. Sargent. It was a great experience for me to see how nice people can be when you are nice to them ... she loved to explain to me exactly what she wanted, and I never questioned her. I was just so proud I could feel almost like an equal. I think how great it was, and is, to be perfectly happy with no thought of self-gain.

You know, I never took a "tip." Even my father could never pay me. It wasn't the tip itself, but I always felt it would ruin my reasons for doing things.

This picture is of our dad, the big "dude" who started the whole thing. Roberto Vittorio (Vitto) could have been the original "Godfather." He was sharp enough to be in that movie. He gave up his possible movie career and status as a tailor to open a grocery store. He claimed business was only sew-sew as a tailor. Many years later he revealed his big secret. He sold everything at "cost". However he bought everything below cost.

Chapter 2

The Swimming Suit

When I was around 12 or 13 years old, I finally started to notice things like what the other kid ate for lunch, how he combed his hair, how he talked, etc. ... and I started to want to do what other people did.

I remember that I wanted to have a swimming suit. We used to go to a bath house called Lurline and they used to give us a little gray swimming piece to swim around with, but I noticed some "rich kids" had these Gattner Mattern suits. (I'm not really sure of the spelling, but I know it sounded like that!)

Anyway, I really wanted this bathing suit, so on Saturday nights I would stay in front of the grocery store and sell the Examiner ... that was the main newspaper in San Francisco at the time, and the Sunday edition cost 10 cents. From this, my father said he would give me the 3-cent profit. Now, **it takes a lot of 3 "centses" to make however much it took to buy this swimming suit!**

I know it is taking me a lot of your time to tell you about a bathing suit ... but it wasn't the swimming suit that was important — it was me. My mother told me much later on in life that when I started in on something, I never finished talking about it until I did it or got it or whatever.

Now, some Saturday nights, I would sit near the papers and I would only sell three in forty minutes. That would be only 12 cents. (Whoops, already I made a mistake!) You know, the biggest weakness I had was math ... I never liked it, I never was going to like it, and I never did like it ... all through life, even today, I don't like math. Now *selling* ... that is something else ... I could sell *anything*! Anyway, back to the bathing suit ... About every three or four sales, I would run into the store and ask my father, "How much do I have for the bathing suit?" This went on and on. My father and mother were really enjoying this at first, because it showed how industrious I was going to be, I think. Then about three Saturdays later, my father kept saying to my mother, "Mary, how much is this bathing suit? Why don't we just buy it for him? I'm so tired of Benny asking how much he has saved up for the suit." Well, **it was the start of a quality which I still have today!**

Chapter 3

Mary, Mary Can't Compare-y

Mary, our mother, was quite a person. All throughout her life, I can't recall her ever saying she was too tired, or she didn't want to have company, or we couldn't help a friend or relative. What a great person, and between her and her mother, Sofia, they lit up more candles, prayed more, and went to St. Peter and Paul's Church more than anyone, it seemed. They kept the Good Lord working overtime, but it was always for a good purpose.

My mother's mother, Sofia, was married in Verbicaro, a small town in a small province called Calabria, which is in Italy. Actually, it was rumored that Calabria was the province where the Mafia originated. **Actually, no one would verify that, as no one wanted that claim to fame!**

Sofia and my grandfather, Beniamino, were married, and their first child was our mother, Mary. **Beniamino decided he was too big to be- little.** He said he wanted a new life in America, so off he went, and he would send for his wife and their little girl, Mary, just as soon as he made good.

Beniamino got a job with a lot of polish and he worked hard to boot in the financial district of San Francisco. He opened his shoe-shine stand with no capital. **The big spenders took a shine to Beniamino** when they heard he was trying to get his wife and daughter to America. They gave him a lot of stock tips, which he kept in his head, as he couldn't speak much English, and he kept the *real* tips to get Sofia and little Mary to America ... **With no principal, but plenty of interest, Beniamino soon had enough capital to send for Sofia and our mother Mary.** Before you could count to seven, there were seven children, who in this order were: Mary, Theresa, Frank, Billy, Tony, Florence, and Vince ... **and that was a pretty big order.** When the kids all grew up, they were still so proud of Tata, they named their children after Beniamino ... he was their idol. It just goes to show you that you didn't have to have a lot of education, you didn't have to have a lot of money, you didn't have to have a lot of looks, but you had to have heart. All you ever need is heart ... and Beniamino and Sofia had that quality for sure.

As our mother Mary grew up, she helped her mother raise part of the family. She received permission to leave school, as the family needed her to help provide. She started working in Chinatown in an art goods store. Her teacher had a good cry when she had to leave school, and so did Mama, but in those days immigrants had to survive.

Soon our grandparents, who started in the North Beach area, found a three-flat home about a mile up. Little did they think Russian Hill would be one of the best areas in all of San Francisco. Later, we were to live in one of the flats. Well, this chapter is about Mary, so we will get back to the store. Mama was never tired ... **she worked 25 hours per day, with one hour off for good behavior,** but she kept going like gangbusters, and she never really complained. The only complaint I ever heard from our mother was about my father's love for gambling. It would follow him throughout his life and whenever she brought it up, my father would say, **"You wanted a Rich and I gave you a Rich** (meaning my brother)." When my father threw away the family money gambling in Reno, my mother said, "Robert threw the money down the toilet." That was the only sour statement she ever made in front of us kids. We were shocked when we heard her say it!

I remember at the store, people would come to the back where Mama would be cooking, just hoping that Mary would ask them to taste what she was making, and she never, ever disappointed them. It was always, "Try my fried eggplant" or "Try my spaghetti, or my meatballs." Now my mother had two types of cooking ... one was the short-cut version that she could cook up in seconds, and then there was the real Mary's version. She could make stuff for an entire family in 30 minutes ... She had a short-cut for any emergency. She had a dried tomato version before anyone ever heard of sun-dried tomatoes. She had short cuts for Italian string beans and potatoes and tomatoes which she made in 20 minutes or so, that I still can't duplicate no matter how hard I try, and neither could anyone else in the family. We had stuffed artichokes that would melt in your mouth, and no matter how many times I try, or ways I try, still no soap ... Mary's were her baby. How could you duplicate the impossible?!!

Our mother could make anything out of fresh vegetables. She had available all the produce that we would have thrown out otherwise at the store, because of lack of refrigeration. She could make any type of salad in minutes with sliced, vine-ripe tomatoes, asparagus, Italian string beans, and olive oil. I guess I will go down to my deathbed dreaming of that type of salad.

I swear half of our business and friends were due to my mother, "Never-say-no Mary." Even our dad, Robert, would say to Mama, "Mary, can't you ever say no?" ... And you know, she *couldn't* say "no."

All of the relatives would visit us — the store was next door to our house — and they would come to buy a lot of produce and fresh fruit, then stay over for dinner. "Zi" meant "auntie" in Italian dialect, and we called every female relative, even if they weren't aunts, Zi Maria, Zi Sofia, etc. Zi Nuzza was my father's sister. She would come over, and we would give her half of the store in fruits and vegetables. She would have dinner, and this relative, Zi Nuzza, was a laugh-a-minute person ... she had lost her husband, but she had four kids; two of the boys, Eddie and Rich, played cards with my brother Rich and me. So Zi Nuzza would gather all of her stuff after dinner and my father would drive her home. My father had another sister, and we called her Zi Mariuch. She was also widowed and lived where the cabbage patches were in San Francisco, at that time ... that part of the city, now known as the Sunset District, was not yet developed ... You could have bought a home there for $2,500.00 ... talk about inflation!!

So, Mary worked in the store at least ten or twelve hours a day, took care of three kids, cooked for one million and a half friends of the store, and never complained. She was a modern-day Jesus, who healed and helped the needy and never turned down anyone.

Mary, Can't Compare-y, cannot be compared to modern women of today. How many can you find that are dedicated to serving everyone else with no thought ever of self-gain? Well, there you have a small part of Mary. When you say Mary was a saint, it is only because you can't think of a better word ... I can: Mother Mary. I know it's two words, but who counts when you know you had the very best mother in the world?!!

This picture proves that my "Dutch" hair cut made my mother make her famous statement that Benny looked a lot cuter. They don't make pictures like this anymore.

Chapter 4

Nana

Today is Easter, a perfect time to tell you about the most Christian person I have ever known — my grandmother, or Nana ... Previously, I mentioned that my mother was Pure ... well, my grandmother was *Pure* Pure ...

Nana lived on Filbert Street, which was on a hill. She lived in a three-flat home, in the flat that was 50 steps up. In those days, I don't think the building code was strict ... because no code today would let you go straight up that many stairs. Now, I said *fifty* steps; **it could have been a few more, but who counts thirty years too late!** God knows how many times a day she went up and down those stairs ... with seven kids, you can imagine how many times it must have been!

Nana went to church almost daily ... she had to pray for somebody, it seemed, every day. She would always say something like, "I'm going to pray for Zia Maria (Auntie Marie)" or "for Zio Giuseppe (Uncle Joe)" ... only we did not use the Zia or Zio, it was Zi ... Zi this or Zi that. Only Calabrese people talked like that ... Calabrese was so different, it did not even come close to real Italian.

Nana loved to talk with her friends in front of St. Peter and Paul's Church. There was always at least a twenty-minute dialogue of who died, who was sick, who was hurt, the whole bit ... Let me give you the English version of what they might say: "You know that man who is the cousin of the brother who is the father-in-law of that girl who lives around the corner from us? Well, that's not the one who's sick — it's his uncle."

Now Nana was about 5 foot 2 with an olive complexion. She had white hair and was neat as a pin. My sister Roberta reminded me that Nana was immaculate and always had a smile on her face ... she was friends with everybody. **Nana loved everyone and no one was exempt.**

Well, Nana spent her day shopping, praying, cooking, and walking up those darn stairs at least 20 times a day. I am sure it gave her long life ... no one knew then how healthy it must have been to do all that exercise.

Now, my grandmother's real name was Sofia and everyone knew Sofia ... I still say my grandmother could have made a fortune suing the Muni Railway

Company in San Francisco. In those days, all we had were street cars ... The E car went down from where we lived to North Beach, stopped one block from St. Peter and Paul's Church, made a right to the Financial District, went all over the City and ended up in the Presidio, which was the military fort in San Francisco. When I say Nana could have been rich, it's because the only times I remember her ever not feeling well were the times she fell or hurt herself on the street car ... but in those days, nobody even thought of liability or suing. Nana just kept rolling along like Ole Man River.

To get to St. Peter and Paul's Church, Nana had to take the E car across the street from our store ... so we got to see her all the time ... always running to get the car ... and it was always somebody's day, like St. Anthony, St. Peter, or a Holy Day of Obligation, Holy Day of Trinity, Holy Day of Something. I used to ask Nana, **"What is today — is it the Holy Day of Matrimony?"** ... She always laughed; I don't think she knew what I was saying, but she laughed because she knew it made me laugh. Nana always had a way of making me laugh.

Later on in life, Nana's children started taking her to Reno or Tahoe when they went on their vacations and they used to give her a couple of rolls of nickels to play the slot machines. She used to say

"JACK-A-POTS" ... She never could say "Jackpots" ... In those days a $7.50 jackpot was pretty good money, at least for Nana!

Nana cooked with a lot of oil. When I used to run up to Nana's, I always asked her if she had made fried potatoes ... they must have been made in a frying pan that could produce the softest, tastiest potatoes in the world ... no matter how my mother tried, they never came out like Nana's ... And she made a lot of other things too — ravioli, tagliarini, 50 kinds of pasta, peppers, sausage ... I remember the sausage used to hang on a dolly in the kitchen until it got real firm — then you could just eat it like jerky ... or she would make it with eggs, and what a dish! For breakfast, lunch, or dinner, her sausage was unique. None of her children could duplicate Nana's cooking; my mother was the oldest child and she was a good cook ... but nobody could beat Nana!

In those days we made something called "conserva," which was made with ground red Anaheim chili peppers that were put in a white cheesecloth bag or an old sugar sack to more or less dehydrate. This would be used in assorted gravies, sausages, and other dishes. Today, I would call it the missing ingredient. Where has it gone? What price tag would an Italian put on being able to find *conserva* today? The modern American housewife would no more be patient enough or have the desire to make this precious recipe.

All the holidays were shared at Nana and Tata's house ... nobody ever tried to say, "We are having Thanksgiving, Easter, or Christmas at our house" ... it was only Nana's. **Too bad the Good Lord couldn't make everyone in his image, but he had a winner with Nana!** Having 30 for dinner was nothing ... and what about the relatives or friends that came *after* dinner! Kissing and hugging was a joke ... it took hours to embrace or kiss, and this went on when people arrived or left, so that took a lot of our time.

Just let me give you an idea of what we would have for a typical holiday meal ... first of all, at Christmas time, there were always Italian *rispedi*, a fried bread dough — at least that was what we called them in Calabrese dialect. Some had red peppers in them and others were plain, but they were fried in olive oil, then kept in a basket, covered, until we ate them. You could heat them again, but they were always good, cold or heated. Imagine, in today's modern world, all you would have to do with *rispedis* is warm them for a minute in the microwave and you would have the finest appetizer that money couldn't even buy!

Anyway, back to the holiday dinners ... we had so many things ... We would start with   peppers in oil, artichoke hearts, white beans in garlic and oil, mushrooms (or "fungi," as we called them) ... then we would have rabbit, just like they make chicken today, then some pasta — sometimes just plain with tomato gravy and sometimes with meat gravy), salad (our salad was just regular lettuce and maybe sliced tomatoes), then leg of lamb or sliced roast beef or veal cutlets, or sometimes all three of them. Then would come the desserts ... cream puffs like in heaven, neapolitans, lady fingers ... Food was not the costliest item in the home ... you could eat like a king and still not hurt the budget ... food was endless! **If there was an Unweight Unwatchers, we belonged to it,** but I guess, today, we would be worried about cholesterol or heart trouble or too much salt ... these days are to be eliminated, but not forgotten, by the survivors.

Today I am thinking of my mother, my grandmother, and my entire family, but most of all, I am thinking of Nana ... **the winner of them all that kept our family glued together by the strongest glue in the world — LOVE.**

When I wrote in the book about Nana, I wasn't kidding. Just look at her face and you can see what an angel she was.

Nana will remain in my memory bank just the way I want to remember God. When she laughed or smiled everyone did the same. When she cried, we all cried. She went to church every day of her life and sometimes twice, but she went to talk to the Good Lord and all of her friends.

Chapter 5

Tata the Big Patata

Tata, or Beniamino, was my grandfather. He raised seven kids and his prior claim to fame was that he had a shoeshine stand in the downtown area ... He was about five foot three and roly poly. He must have brought home about twenty or thirty dollars per week, tops, but Tata dominated the scene. It was the way he was loved, obeyed, and looked up to that did it. When Tata came home, all of us ran to the door. When Tata talked, we listened.

In front of Tata's stand was a gumball machine. Now, according to how it worked, one penny got you one to three gumballs ... all bright colors like red, blue, yellow, and green, but the most popular color was black, or licorice. Now, I hated black, but because all the other kids wanted black, I made believe I liked it. Being part of our family, Tata's gambling instinct made him always try to get the three gumballs for a penny ... but his minimum take-home was always at least one for each of us kids.

Remember that Nana ran up and down those stairs about twenty or thirty times a day ... Tata only did it twice, once going down and once coming up ... but there was a bannister, and he would grab that and chug upstairs. We would all kiss him and follow him into the kitchen. He had a little wooden barrel filled with claret wine ... One drink would send a normal person reeling, but Tata always finished it, once per day, and in 10 or 15 minutes he would fall asleep.

He had a strap which he would threaten us with if we misbehaved and we would scatter like mice when he snapped it against the table ... Fortunately, he never carried out his threat on any of us, but being young kids, we always got scared when he made believe he was angry.

Tata would give each of his kids a box of Wrigley's chewing gum to sell in the park ... there was Uncle Frank, Uncle Bill, Uncle Tony and Uncle Vince ... Vince, believe it or not, was born one year before my brother, Rich ... so we were all raised together.

Now, to get back to my favorite part of this memory — the gumballs. I really liked orange, but everyone fought for the black gumball. With all the wealth and things in life, why does this stand out in my memory? ... It just goes to show how complex life is ... **just when you think you know something, you find out you don't.**

One day, my mother told her father (our grandfather) that we could use him at the store in the mornings. You can imagine his feelings! Now, at 6:00 a.m., how many customers could you get?! But we had advertised that we were open from 6:00 a.m. to 10 p.m. and that's the way it was going to be ... so Tata was it! He would get to the store even earlier than 6:00 a.m., but that was *his* store and *he* was running it. I don't know how much he took in, but it was probably less than five or ten dollars. I always wondered about what he charged, because all he really knew about was milk and bread and that is what most people needed that early in the morning. **I figured, if they bought something big, Tata would charge more than if they bought something small, but that was the chance we took.**

There was a basement in the store, and Tata took it upon himself that, even after my mother or father got to the store, he would run the basement ... so with a series of orange and apple crates, he built shelves and stocked all the extra canned goods from the store. He made a sign that said "Tata's." A lot of times, he would fall asleep after lunch and then go home about 2:00 or 3:00 in the afternoon. Tata was proud of his work in the store, and now he could tell his Italian friends in North Beach and in Italy that he was promoted from shoeshine expert to inventory manager in a grocery store!

Tata was truly the Big Patata ... the big potato ... he may have been small, but he was plenty big. Again, in fact, he was too big to be little. When God made our Tata, he broke the mold!

Tata had it all. Look at this picture. Could you believe he ran a shoe shine stand in the financial district of San Francisco. He worked for pennies to get his wife to America. Later we hired him for the early morning hours shift at the grocery store. When Tata talked, we listened!

Chapter 6

Berkeley Bobby

In the beginning, before my family bought the store in San Francisco, we lived in Berkeley at 1318 Woolsey Street, a few blocks away from our Uncle Dave's house. **Our house was the type of home they sold to people that had no money ... like nothing down and two to go.**

My father was a partner in Galileo Market in San Francisco at the time, and he took the ferry to San Francisco and back every morning and night.

Here is the beginning of what I remember ... I remember the train used to stop at Woolsey Street. I remember that. I remember my mother used to buy us Wrigley's gum when we took the train. It came out of a little gum machine. You put in a nickel and, according to what seat you had, that's the kind of gum that came out ... it was either Juicy Fruit (my favorite), Spearmint, or Doublemint (my non-favorite). We kids always wanted Juicy Fruit and my mother took Doublemint, as most older people would. All that, I remember. I remember my mother used to yell from our house and ask for us to come home. We were a gathering of about five to eight little kids, and I was the storyteller. I was the talker in this little group. I would tell "spooky" stories, and **this little group would listen to me, as if I were Jesus and this was my flock.** In the beginning, this was how it was ... I could hold court with these little kids.

Nowadays, a mother would not dare let her children out after it got dark ... but back then, there was absolutely no fear of anything bad happening; no ... mothers had plenty to do without fear. The only fear was of making a living and surviving.

My mother, my brother Rich, and I had all kinds of fun with Uncle Dave's wife, Antonette, and her children. We used to like to go to Neptune Beach, which was in Alameda. Antonette was the only driver and they had a Model T Ford. It was a little car, but we all squeezed in and drove to Neptune Beach ...

At that time, their children consisted of Bobby and Gene, and there was Richie and me ... so the six of us would head for Neptune Beach ... Now Bobby was the first born of Antonette and Dave, and for some unknown reason, Bobby was not talking until he was four or five. My mother worked with Bobby and got him talking. **We used to ask Bob, later in life, how come he didn't talk until he was about**

age five, and his answer (now a joke) was that until that time everything was O.K.

Later, when Bob was older, say about my age, as he and I were both born on August 9th, Bob came to stay with us for one whole summer, at our house on Filbert Street. Bob talks about this like he was in heaven. He can remember every little thing we did, every place we went, everything we ate ... you name it and Bobby remembers it. But that isn't what I'm trying to tell you; it is the way he goes through it all, almost as if he were hypnotized. If you ever wanted to get drunk and cry in your beer, Bobby would be the guy to be with, because he makes bread into cake, cake into ice cream and so on down the line ... and you know what? As he is telling you all this, he is in a reverent state ... oh, how I wish I could have that quality! One of Bob's special memories was my mother's Spaghetti Pie ... he would and could talk about it like it was a miracle recipe that no one else in the world knew how to make. I did a little investigation, and you know something? ... No one in our entire family could make it as my mother could. I'm not sure if it was the oil or the spaghetti. My mother used left-over spaghetti, eggs that were freshly scrambled, and olive oil, and put it in a big, big frying pan ... then she would cook it slowly and when it was ready on the bottom she had a big dish and she would put the dish on top, turn the spaghetti over to the other side, and finish cooking it ... now, no one knows if it was the fact that the spaghetti was leftover, or if she had any magic other than the way she made it. All we know is that no one in the entire family could ever duplicate this delicacy.

Now, Uncle Dave was a shoe repair man; however, he developed a great arch support that became famous, and people rich or poor, near or far, came to Uncle Dave to have it made ... it was, at that time, one of the finest cures for bad or aching backs. He had a following. I developed a bad back some time after the War, and went to Uncle Dave. It was fun to watch Uncle Dave's process. First he made you take off your shoes. Then he got a marking pencil and asked you questions about where your back hurt and how you developed your troubles, so he would know how to carve leather arch supports and how to divide and conquer, and *voila* — he would say to come back in a week and he would have the solution. I can't tell you how many rich and famous people in San Francisco Uncle Dave could say he cured. He was the forerunner of things to come in that specialized field. He cured my back and, could you believe, I still have those leather arch supports that Uncle Dave carved for me when I had my first "bad back" incident.

We recently went to an Italian picnic for Italians who were born in Calabria or raised from Calabria-born parents, and who should be there but Gene and Bob and their families! All of our parents had passed away, and Bob started in with all these stories. We spent hours listening to things that only Bob could remind us of. I had made some sandwiches that consisted of a french roll, cream cheese, and red peppers that had been roasted in olive oil. You know, a year later, he was again telling everyone in the picnic grounds about my famous pepper sandwiches, so by the time lunches were brought out, my famous peppers, cut in two now to meet my new popularity (developed by Bobby), were all gone. It reminded me of when Jesus started with only a few loaves of bread and was able to satisfy 6,000 people ... Oh well, only Bobby, son of David, could have developed this popularity for me!

I guess in those days it was possible, with very little money, but a heart filled with joy, to have fun and memories. To our Uncle Dave and his family, we salute them. Only Lorraine, one younger child of Antonette and Dave, and our sister Roberta, or Bert, were not mentioned in this chapter, as they came later and they probably have their own stories to tell. For now, the Berkeley Boy, Bobby, and Benny have August 9th to remember us by ... What is your claim to fame?

As it was, it was Roberta that reminded me about our mother getting Bobby to talk, and it was Bobby that reminded me of the spaghetti pie, so you see, **I know very little except that I forgot to remember** ... Ah, I remember it well ... no, that is in another chapter!

Berkeley Bobby was something else. He could make silver into gold, milk into ice cream... when he was through with you, you missed the best party, the best football game, and the best meal to eat. If you ever wanted to get drunk, he would be the guy you would want with you. Yep!!!, Bobby was really something else!

Chapter 7

Monday Night

When Rich and I got a little older, we told our parents we would work in the store on Monday nights, so they could take the evening off. Rich and I, and the gang of kids that helped and worked in the store, would work until 9:00 p.m. Then we would be allowed hot chocolate with cookies for our treat. What started as nothing, ended up great. Our mother and father would go to a movie at the Alhambra Theater, only two blocks away on Polk Street. That theater is still there today, 60 years later.

Monday night was a slow night for the theater, so they had Bank Night, with prizes and free dishware. My parents could not believe their good luck, and we kids had lots of laughs, with jokes and small talk. The kids that worked with us all loved the comraderie of those days.

My father usually had three or four kids about our age working in the store. My parents would choose kids from poor families or whose fathers had died. They would give the kids $5.00 per week and we would load up the kids with all the fruit and vegetables they could carry home. You must remember, there was no refrigeration in those days ... better to see a poor family with food and a sense of honor that their sons were helping.

I usually ended up with that crew of kids. As I told you before, my brother Rich would be at the cash register and he had the keys to close the store. He was allowed to drive our old jalopy truck, as the State of California Motor Vehicle Department allowed him to drive at 14 years of age. There was no traffic to speak of in those days ... nobody except businesses or rich families had cars ... We are talking 1931 or 1932 or so ...the heart of the Depression. My little gang of kids would go down to the basement where my grandfather worked with the canned goods.. .then we would restock the shelves with the canned foods until 9:00 p.m.

All of us kids were growing. My father's sister was widowed and had four children — Richie, Peter, Eddie, and Florence. We grew up with Eddie and Richie and had a card game for pennies on Sundays, as we were learning to play poker. Eddie worked in the store from around that time until he got married. We used to send Eddie home with boxes of produce ... in this way, my parents never made the relatives or close friends feel they were getting charity; this kept everyone happy. Remember, these were deep Depression days. **What did I know about**

depressions? Jimmy Durante used to say, "What is a depression? It's a dent. What's a dent? It's a hole. What is a hole? It's nothing ...so we don't have anything to worry about!"

Without our family realizing it, we started to be leaders among our group of relatives. My dad bought the property next door ... two flats for $10,000. He bought a used electric player piano with all the rolls. No one had to push the pedals like on the old player pianos, so we could all follow the music ... We had all the Irving Berlin tunes and catchy songs from other writers, too ... we had "Baby Face," "Yes, We Have No Bananas," "You Made Me Love You," "Barney Google, with the Goo Goo Googlie Eyes," ... we had lots of fun, as all the kids were our age and they loved to come to our house.

My mother never tired of cooking, and the grown-ups would eat tons of spaghetti, lasagna, veal scallopini, ravioli, and just about every other Italian dish. The mothers would bring us kids sandwiches in the living room, and we would eat in there while the grown-ups ate in the kitchen. After dinner, the men would play "Pedro," a popular card game, in the dining room, while the women would clean up and talk, happy to be happy.

My parents enjoyed being able to be of help in these terrible times. Many years afterwards, we would realize what a depression was and were glad it was over and that many people went back to work.

There was one thing for sure: Unless you knew the names of the members of my father's "Pedro Club", you could not figure out who was who. My father was "Duck Feet"; my Uncle Tony was "Wildcat", my Uncle Billy was "Bronco Billy"... Then there was "Sleepy Joe", "The Turk", and "Silver-Tip". These were just a few that I remember and for over fifty years they played Pedro every Tuesday night. You could count on one hand how many Tuesdays they missed. It was arguments by the minute, but friendships forever.

Chapter 8

The Game Before The Game

One of the fascinating enjoyments of our family life was the Pedro Card Club. In those days, "Pedro" was not as known as it is today, but for fifty years we had the Pedro Club in the weekly family schedule. I don't believe in fifty years anyone ever missed more than a few nights, and I can't recall them ever calling off the game. They may have switched the date, but the actual game carried on. Now remember, this is not me talking, but I was a boy growing up and once every twelve weeks the game was at our house. That was the day I was sure to stay home to watch. Now let me tell you a secret. That was not the game I wanted to watch; *it was the game before the game that had us spellbound.*

Now before I get to that excitement, let me tell you a little about the make-up of the Pedro Club in my father's time. There were approximately twelve members, and maybe two fill-ins that were waiting for a member to get sick or drop out or temporarily not be able to play. They were 99% Italian and all Calabrese. As I mentioned before, Calabria was a small province in Italy, rumored to be the original home of the Mafia. **The original Mafia was**

**rumored to be a group that kicked the bad guys
out of Italy and nobody knows nothing**, just like
in "The Godfather". Anyway, one of the twelve
original guys was one that they called an "American."
They called him "Skinny Nose." He was not Italian.
**They almost all had nicknames, I guess to protect
the "innocent."**

Believe it or not, this club lasted fifty years. There
are only three members alive today: one is our Uncle
Tony; another is a cousin, Sleepy Joe; and the last is
another cousin, Louie. In an interview with Uncle
Tony, he remembered everything about the Pedro
game, but was hazy about the other game. But it is
the game before the other game that is the "fun" part
of the story.

There may be some relatives or Calabrese Italians
that will remember this and what I am going to tell,
but believe me, I have been unable to track it down
as yet. Just my luck, when the book comes out, some
nut will remember everything and ruin my story!

Here goes. The name of the game was called
Briscala or it could have been "Brischala," as the
"h" is silent in Italian. Most of the members knew
how to play the game. The ones that arrived early to
the home where the Pedro game was to be played
would have the luxury of playing their home town

or their parents' home town favorite game of Briscala. Here is where we little kids would really laugh. It was so funny, you would think you were in a psychopathic ward of a hospital or, as we called it, "the crazy house."

The game was played with four players, two partners against two partners. The important cards were the two threes of the trump suit. Other key cards were the Kings, Queens and Jacks. The threes counted as 10 points and other points were the Aces, Kings, Queens, and Jacks. I believe the Kings were four points, the Jacks were three points and the Queens were two points. Hey, what's the exact difference?... that wasn't the part of the story that is or was important. The SIGNALS were the key to the game. Each partner was facing each other and the opposition was facing each other. Quickly, after the first cards were dealt, each party had three cards.

Now get ready for the part that broke all of us kids up, the signals. The blinking of the right eye was the trump three card. The other eye was the second highest card. Now if the trump was spades, the other black three was the next best card. Somehow that was the game. Now we come to more signals. The King was the raising of your eyebrows, the Queen was sticking out your tongue, and the Jack was the moving of your shoulders. We might find out much later life in life the exact points, but it won't matter. There were false signals all the time, where one partner signals he has a "three" and, in a flash, shakes his head, so you never knew what was what; the player might not throw a point card out. Then again, they had counter-signals and counter-counter signals and, being the partners were facing each other, the other partner kept missing the changes or the non-important changes in the game.

If you ever saw a game of this type, you could not stop laughing… it was sheer ectasy for a kid like me to watch my father in action. Now remember, the real Italians like my father, who were born in Calabria, were a lot different. My uncles were all born in America… these old timers could run rings around the newborn Calabrians, believe me. Now we that were spectators had all the fun.

The game was played for about fifty cents a player and that was years later, when inflation changed the amounts that were at stake. What I would give now to be able to see these old-timers play a game! Imagine that there are only three living from the days I saw the real game of Briscala or Brischala being played. I don't care how you spell it, but you would be "spell-bound" to see that fun game being played. Like the old-timers say when they get together, "They don't play games like that anymore." One final note:

there were No 8's, 9's and 10's. So there were only 40 cards in the game. So Cards 40, where are you???

This was another picture of the San Francisco Pedro Club. Here they are all dressed up, as the affair was held at the 365 Club, famous at that time for food and fun and entertainment.

Chapter 9

Gamblers Unanimous

I guess it's about time we talked about the head of our family. My mother called him Robert, my grandmother called him Roberto, and his children called him Pa or Papa. His salesman and business friends called him Bob.

From the stories that our mother told us, our father was a gambler. He loved to play cards and, in fact, he was playing cards across the street in North Beach when Richie was born. My grandmother told Roberto if he didn't shape up she would take her daughter back.

Papa came from Calabria, Italy, from a town called Verbicaro ... The Calabrese people are from southern Italy. **He was a tailor by trade, so he traded it in for a grocery store.** The name of the store was Galileo Market, a good Itralian name and fitting for my parents ... still today, this market is in business on Polk Street, after 60 years.

My father loved to gamble ... It never let him down and he enjoyed it his entire life. Although it cost him money, what else in life was more fun! My parents were like the government ... when my father made money, it went through all the relatives and close friends — **it certainly was a trickle-down family!** We had so many kids work in our store for $5.00 a week, but they took home $100.00 worth of produce. My parents gave away just as much or more of what they made, only they gave it away in food. **And in the Great Depression, what more could you want but food for the family!**

By the time Rich and I got to be 10 or 12 years of age, the store in Russian Hill was producing profits. Rich and I were in Spring Valley Grammar School, which was six blocks away from the store. I guess that would have been about 1929 to 1931 or somewhere around that time — right about the time of the Crash ...**The Crash heard around the world was never, ever brought up.**

Papa liked action and he got it when he bought the store. He had many rich customers and they all liked my dad ... He could get along with the so-called famous "big shots." On my mother's side it was all family ... **we had relations coming out of our ears; we had relations all over the City.**

Well, the grocery store brought prosperity, but we could never hold on to anything like that ... we had constant company; my father hired every relative's son that could need or could carry home produce for his family ... we were like the government trying to help the needy ... so what?! ... **easy come, easy go ... we helped everyone that needed it.**

While the store brought good news, our father would go to Reno to distribute some of his wealth. Harold Smith of Harold's Club was on a first name basis with my father Bob ... My dad had credit in days when there was no credit. Remember, you could buy a home for $1,000 to $2,000 in those days. My father never complained, never cried sour grapes, never asked for help ... but his mind worked miracles. He knew more about buying than I'll ever know about baseball or football ... it was like second nature to him. He could get melons that were selling for 50 cents for only 5 cents ... Don't ask me how, but he could see where money could be made, with just a twist of the wrist ... **When he was in need, he was brilliant indeed.**

Later on in life, as my uncles on my mother's side got older, they all played pinochle. With three or four around, they could always get up a game. It was fun to watch them ... they always played like they were playing for millions, even if it was for 25 cents a game and 10 cents a set. To them it was the challenge. You could hear them saying, "Mary, one more minute — I think I have Bob set," or "Florence, (the youngest daughter in my grandmother's house), turn on the

light in the hallway — we'll be right there for dinner."
You know, if you saw them, you would think it was
the end of the world ... but a few minutes later they
were all eating together, talking about the horses.

My father never did like the horses and told my
uncles how stupid they were playing the sucker's
horse races ... however, many years later, when the
big War was on, he started to play $2.00 on the horses
out of boredom. He never played with his heart in it.
He always played the long shots, saying, "You can't
win playing for $3.00 when you only get $2.00." He
was right, but he never won with his system either.
They used to argue about all this and plenty more
that never amounted to anything — but what a
household! Never a dull moment at Nana and Tata's
house. A few minutes after one of these arguments,
you could hear the guys singing songs like "Yes, We
Have No Bananas," "If You Knew Suzie," or "That
Old Gang of Mine." If you were a stranger, you
would not believe it.

My mother's three oldest brothers were Frank,
Bill, and Tony. Frank died later in life, all dressed
up with a racing form in his pocket, ready to go to
the track. Billy died at Lake Tahoe, getting ready to
go to the clubs to gamble. Tony is still living and
plays cards with me, my son, my brother-in-law, and

four other nuts. Yeah, who said I wasn't crazy like my father?!!

Too bad we found all those ways of losing money, but gambling seemed to be in our family — baseball games, later on pro-football games. All you would hear was, "I had 60 to 1 on the last game of the season," "New York lost," or whatever. Nobody seemed to talk about worldly affairs ... only my father; he knew plenty about what was going on in the world.

My brother Rich and I used to play baseball cards when we were little and he would always win. I would cry and Mama would make him give them all back to me. Anyway, Rich could drive the truck; I couldn't. Rich knew mathematics like he invented it; I couldn't add 27 and 34 without writing it down and then figuring it out. Rich had wavy hair and I had straight hair. Rich was good-looking and I thought I wasn't. Rich could play the piano or hit or catch a baseball better than I could. Rich was sharper than I was. **But outside of that, I had more charisma than he did, because my mother said so — and she was the boss!**

Mama always tried to even up the score. When we ate in the back of the store, Papa would start his mathematical talk about percentages and would say, "A man paid $2,000 for a store and he sells it for

$3,000. What percentage profit would he make?"
Richie always knew the answer. My father never
did understand how I felt. My mother would always
interject that Benny was the best talker in the family
and that he was going to be a famous lawyer someday.
Oh well, I never improved in math and my mother
would put her arms around me from behind and say,
"That's all right, Benny; you are going to be the
lawyer in the family. Nobody talks like you." I
wonder what she meant by that!

I remember when I told my father that I wanted to
buy the store kitty-corner from our store when I grew
up and my father told me, "Go to college. When
you come back, if you want a store like that, I'll buy
you two of them."

Do you know I was the first one of all my 400
relatives that ever graduated from college? Now,
we have doctors, lawyers, etc., but at that time nobody
even had the encouragement or the money to go to
or finish college.

My father was light years ahead of any of our
relatives, but gambling was his big weakness. He
would bet on rain, sunshine, baseball, football, cards,
etc., but his big costly weakness was dice ... he could
lose it at Harold's Club, come home, talk about
anything else, but not about losing ... he was the best

loser Harold's Club ever had. But think about it —
what else was around at that time? What a boring
life, I guess, without taking a chance. Look at the
lotteries and gambling casinos today — that will tell
you my father was way ahead of his time.

Many years later, after the War, I came home and
there was my father with some of the relatives in the
dining room playing poker. I heard my father say, "I
raise you one penny." I thought back to the times
my father probably said, "I raise you $10.00," or even
$100.00, and thought nothing of it. You see, it wasn't
the amount of money ... it was the fun of life. No,
my father wasn't playing for pennies. My father
didn't live for money; he lived for sharing and
enjoying family life. Papa was solid gold!

Chapter 10

Take Me Out to the Old Brawl Game

I am on a roll today, so I thought I would sit down and **you can figure out if I am on a Jelly Roll, a Tootsie Roll, or a real roll** ... let me know later. You know, **as they say in French, "Tooth Sweet"; or in Mexican talk, "Hot Today, Chile Tamale."** I forgot to tell you that our entire family, including my uncles Frank, Billy, Tony, and Vince, all loved the San Francisco Seals, now known as the San Francisco Giants. We would go out to the ball park, mostly on weekends, to see the Seals play. We would be allowed in free, or for a nickel or a dime, to watch the games. It was always fun.

My uncles played a lot of semi-pro or Sunday ball. On Sundays in San Francisco, there were a lot of games sponsored by different commercial interests, who bought the uniforms and spent the money for local publicity. My Uncle Frank managed a local club called Olympic Florist. They actually won the championship one season, which made all of us very proud.

Many famous players like Joe DiMaggio, Tony Lazzeri, Dino Restelli, Beans Marionetti, Gino

Cimoli, Frank Crossetti, Dominic DiMaggio, Dario Lodigiani, and my cousin Frank Lucchesi — all Italian — all went up to the Big Leagues. San Francisco was a spawning ground, as many kids did not even have a high school education. **Joe DiMaggio went to Galileo High School for about two hours, then left to go commercial fishing with his father** ... oh, those were the Depression years all right!

DiMaggio astounded the baseball world when he hit in 61 straight games in a row. After that kind of a year, he was picked up by the Yankees and became probably the greatest known player in the game.

We used to go out to Seals Stadium and I could hardly wait to get a "Hot Air." It was similar to the now-known famous Milky Way, but it was frozen, and it cost five cents ... oh, to chew on that bar until it finally melted in your mouth was a kid's dream. The candy company that made them was the forerunner of companies like Scoreboard or Topps, and made black-and-white baseball cards with a coupon on the bottom. There were no colored baseball cards in those days. You could trade in your coupons for baseball gloves, spikes, bats, and other baseball equipment. In fact, I got my first baseball glove with their coupons.

We used to play to win them from each other, in order to accumulate them for the prizes. They had three products to get the cards from ... One was called Home Run Kisses, and that was a box of taffy; another was Ruf-Nek, and that was Rocky Road; and the last one was Zee Nut, which was similar to Cracker Jacks. Now believe it or not, these cards were the forerunners of the card craze to hit the country after the WWII. If I had my cards today, I would be a millionaire ... guys like Paul Waner, Ted Williams, Joe DiMaggio, Lefty O'Doul — you name him and, if he was great, the chances are he went up to the Big Leagues from the Pacific Coast League.

Now, here was the way we played the cards: one was simply matching; you flipped the card from your hip and it settled down in a heads or tails manner ... if you matched the card your opponent had thrown, you won his card. In another game, you threw your cards against the wall and the one who threw the card closest to the wall won the cards ... two or three could play at a time ... if you got a card against the wall standing up, it was the best you could get; a card that leaned against the wall was called a "leaner" and was second best; and, finally, the third best was when your card touched the wall — that generally was enough to win. Wow ... I would like to have my old cards back ... I wouldn't be writing this book; I would be counting all my money instead!

Take me out to the Old Brawl Game, we used to call it in our family, as a lot of those games turned out to be brawls ...

Remember, I told you about my brother Richie and me playing those cards? My brother would always win and then the water works would start; I would always cry and then my mother would make my brother give me back my cards. I don't remember ever beating Rich, and I will tell you one thing — it made a great person out of me ... **losing is not a bad thing if it improves your style or your habits or your personality.** I never gave up, and my poor mother never gave up telling me I was going to be the lawyer in the family. Why she always said that, I'll never know for sure, but I think it was my ability to create situations and talk better than anyone in the family.

In my next book, I will tell you what competition did for me in the business world. One thing I will accept: I liked trying to get out of situations or jams; I liked speaking out; and, best of all, I liked to write. I could write all day, and even from scratch I could create. Like Al Jolson always said, "You ain't seen nothin' yet."

Now, you probably thought Rich could run rings around me, but **the only rings around me were run**

by my sister, Roberta, and that was in Ring-Around-the-Rosie ...only kidding, folks, and this is the end of me foolin' around for this chapter ... Next chapter, I will be all business.

Chapter 11

Growing Up

Soon we were growing up. High school was a great experience for me, as I started to expand my ability to talk more. Rich was ahead of me by 17 months. The school we were going to had two sessions, as San Francisco was having a school shortage, so we would get out of school by noon ... We would hurry to the store to work.

I couldn't wait to work on the produce section of the store, and, remember, the deli section had to be cleaned up ... I used to love to decorate the produce and make designs with the different color vegetables, such as yellow squash next to the green squash, or red bell peppers near the white cauliflower. I liked everything about the business — the store, my waiting on customers ... We were growing fast and I was involved in all of that. **Life is great when you don't realize the troubles in the world.**

I was always thinking of funny signs to put around the store. I remember, one day I put a sign in the window that read: **"PRESS THIS WINDOW RIGHT HERE AND FEEL THE PAIN."** With our friendly store, all the people were coming in saying, "I didn't feel any pain." And I would say, "You didn't feel the WINDOW PANE?"

Then I would tell them, **"A guy stepped on an orange peel in the store today and we had to give him orange-aid."** No matter what or how they answered, I would say, **"Now, Orange Juice sorry I told that joke?".** I always thought I should have been a comedian, just for laughs.

Well, I was growing up and still a little self-conscious. I was dark-complected and had very straight hair ... nothing I could do would put it down. Like I told you in a previous chapter, **my brother Rich had wavy hair and was a handsome guy ... but I could use some help.** Rich was also more coordinated, played better sports, and could beat me at almost anything ... You know, that would help me later in life ... you see, I wanted to be good at something, so in my senior year at high school, I got active in journalism and became the sports reporter for the school newspaper.

Without knowing it, I started to change. I started to change the school sports page. I started to join school clubs and became president of the Italian Club and the Commercial Club. I started going to the school dances. **Oh, I was changing all right ... even my parents started noticing their little Benny.** They gave me time off from the store to cover the football games, plus time off for the senior dances.

My aunt Florence taught me how to dance a little. In those days, no one danced anything but a two-step. **Gee, I didn't even know ... maybe there was a three-step or a four-step, too!** Who ever dreamed of a tango, or a waltz, or something complicated?

I was scared stiff of girls, having no prior experience. Soon I figured out that if I had a little talking patter, the girls would laugh and maybe forget I was not good-looking or whatever. (I would like to interject that, I guess, I was actually a fairly good-looking kid, but at the time, I did not think so ... after all, **I used to tell the girls I was "Tall, Dark, and Hands-off!"**) So, when dancing with a girl I would say, **"Hi, did you know my parents were in the Iron and Steel business? My mother irons and my father steals."** Then I would follow with something like, **"I call my girlfriend my melancholy baby ... she has a head like a melon and a face like a collie."** Once I had them laughing, I would start to relax.

It was a great experience to find out that I could mingle with the girls and the upper set. In fact, I used to end my little routine up with, **"I used to travel with the upper set. Next week I'm having my lowers put in."**

We had a "mock" store in our annual album at Galileo High School. There I am with my store gown, waiting on a customer.

I was seventeen years old. When it came to the store, I was always happy. Maybe I just loved to talk to people. I worked throughout the four years I spent in college. And even after the War, I put some time into my dad's new store.

Chapter 12

The Zoot Suit

When I was about 16 or 17 years of age, I had a big desire to get me a "real live" suit. I was coming into my own, going to the school senior dances, and I was building up a little reputation with my writings for the sports page and my creative work in that field. I was thinking now that I should have a suit, because suppose I had to go out or they were taking pictures for the school yearbook ... I needed to look my best.

In those days, in San Francisco, or S.F., or the City, as we called it, the best store to buy a suit was Roos Brothers ... nothing ever was on sale, but it was the best men's store to buy clothes. All the kids would judge your coat by looking at the inside, to see if it had the Roos Brothers' label. Why it was that all the kids were so concerned with looking for the labels on the inside of your coat was a mystery to me. One of my favorite jokes was to say **I had a suit that was half cotton and half rotten** ... or I would say **my suit was all wool, except the zipper.**

Now there was a new store in the Bay Area; it was a chain store type operation called Forman & Clark Clothing Store. This store advertised "Upstair

Shopping with Downstair Prices." It featured bargain prices and two pairs of trousers with each suit. Roos Brothers never made any of these gimmick offers.

I had seen this suit, say for about $34.00, in the window, where a suit at Roos Brothers was $50.00 or $60.00 ... In those days, people were lucky if they had one suit. Anyway, I saw this suit in the window. It was gabardine and it was blue, but it seemed to have a twinge of purple in the color of the fabric. Why it appealed to me, I have no idea ... in today's world you would have to be crazy, or you would be embarrassed to own this suit ... but 17 years of age and a new confident Benny made me buy it. And don't forget that I would get two pairs of trousers with the suit ... this was a new innovation in selling.

At that time, there was a very famous band leader called Ben Bernie ... he talked like a Southern person and always ended all his programs by saying, "Yowsah, yowsah, yowsah." ... So I created a joke of mine that **I just bought a Ben Bernie suit ... one with two pairs of yowsahs.** Another joke I used to tell was, **"It took five men to make my suit — Forman and Clark."**

Anyway, I bought the Forman & Clark suit, took off the label from the inside, sewed on a Roos Brothers' label from one of my father's old suits, and *voila*! ... I was wearing what the well-dressed 16 or 17 year old was!

In those days, a person was lucky to have a suit of clothes. This was actually my second suit, as my parents had bought me one for my confirmation. **I called that my holy suit ... I bought it at a fire sale ... Holy Smoke!**

So this was the story of my Zoot Suit. I wore it for quite awhile, but as I got older, I realized it wasn't going to get me into Hollywood to have a suit like that. My father, who had been a tailor, bought me a new suit from Roos Brothers, with the real Roos Brothers' label, for my high school graduation.

You know something? That suit taught me something. What it was I'll never know, but **when I see someone with a lousy suit on, I always say, "There by the grace of God could have been me."**

Chapter 13

"One Polk and Two Fell ..."

Five times I have sat down to write, and five times nothing ... how can I produce anything when I have Polk Street on my mind?!! What is Polk Street? It's really a nothing street, but to me it was one of my great childhood memories. **No matter what side of the street you were on, it was the "sunny side of the street"** and a block that I will never block out of my memory bank. As the great San Francisco Chronicle writer, Herb Caen, always said, "There is a **One Polk and Two Fell** address somewhere in San Francisco!"

Let us analyze Polk Street ... The bus starts right at San Francisco Bay. Polk Street was important because whether you were coming or going, you saw some of the most important places in San Francisco on both sides. **If you've heard Tony Bennett sing "I Left My Heart in San Francisco," you've been to Polk Street.** That song tells it all.

The first stop is San Francisco Bay, where you have Fisherman's Wharf. What a place! Eat all the crab or shrimp you want, all the prawns and other kinds of fish ... **They have everything you could want in seafood. All you have to do is pay ... the rest is free!**

The views at Fisherman's Wharf were outstanding (and if you were not careful, they might let you stay out standing!). You could see Yacht Harbor, the Marina Greens, and, two blocks beyond, my future alma mater: Galileo High School. Then, of course, there was Coit Tower and our family favorite, "Freddy's Sandwich Shop," which I will tell you more about in a later chapter. You could even see the Golden Gate and Bay Bridges, with boats sailing under them almost every minute. All this, and you've only gone two blocks! Another block or so and you have the "crookedest" street in the world: Lombard Street. And above that block, you could see Berkeley, Alcatraz Island, and all the ferry boats.

Coming along, we find Ghiradelli Chocolate Factory. They made every chocolate you could imagine, day and night. **I heard that "chocoholics" could pass by, inhale, and still gain five pounds!**

Just a block or so further and you hit Galileo Market, the first grocery store my father owned; it is still there today, run by its third owner. My grandmother's house was a couple of blocks to the left, and if you continued in that direction, you would reach St. Peter & Paul's Catholic Church, where Nana practically lived. **She went 99 days out of 98 (sometimes she went twice a day!)** Once there was a fire at the church and I asked her, **"Nana, what did you say when you saw the fire?"** ... Nana's reply was, **"Holy smoke!"**

Continuing up Polk Street, we come to the famous Alhambra Theater, which was built in the movie era, and is still standing on Polk Street. It was written up in the Hollywood magazines as one of the finest, and the "Last of the Mohicans" of the great movie palaces. We never called them "theaters" in those days ... we all called them "shows." Every kid would say, "I'm going to the show today." It was there that I received my Mickey Mouse badge. I was one of the first ones chosen to represent the Mickey Mouse Club. I used to say, **"This is no Mickey Mouse operation; it's the real thing!"** How can we forget the likes of Hoot Gibson, Tom Mix, Will Cody, Dustin Farnum, Frankie Darro, plus the greatest dog in movie history, Rin Tin Tin ... Those serials kept you going back every Saturday for years and years.

Right next to the Alhambra was a candy store that started me in my gambling career. They used to show you a box of chocolate-covered mints with maybe eighty in a box. You had to pick one out, and if the center was pink instead of white, you got a large candy bar to eat in the show. Anyway, I figured out how to win the candy bar ... evidently, they double-dipped the ones with the pink centers so you couldn't see the pink ... and that was the clue. I would pretend I was looking over the box of mints, and after about thirty seconds I would pick one (of course the one that looked double-dipped!) ... wow! A winner! **Imagine the brains I had, to break this ring of chocolate minters!** Oh, I almost forgot to mention that, to try to win the nickel candy bar, each mint cost one cent. **How I could leave out that important detail just doesn't make any cents!** Oh well, it was great to be a kid on Polk Street!

Our house and grocery store (the one that you have read so much about in this book) were two blocks up from the Alhambra Theater, on Union Street. We kids used to love to run over to Polk Street, whenever we got a chance.

Next, coming up Polk Street, was the Helen Wills Playground, named after the popular women's tennis champion. It became the home of so many champions.

Gracing this playground were the likes of Joe DiMaggio and Hank Luisetti, the father of the push shot. I can't tell you how many "Itralian" stars got their starts in that I playground. I used to go there and hope that someone would pick me as a substitute for something. **I was the best "non-picked" guy that ever was "non-picked" to play anything they ever had. I had lots of memories of not playing with the best of them!**

Yes, Polk Street was right in the middle of all this great action. Business was good for all the stores on either side of the street. These stores were starting to advertise in the shopping newspapers. My father always told the story of the lady that came in his store to complain that his strawberries were too expensive, that down on Polk Street they were three baskets for only twenty cents ... so my father said to this lady, "Why don't you go down to Polk Street and buy them?" She answered, "Oh, they are closed on Sundays." My father's reply was, **"When I'm closed, I sell them for three for a nickel!"**

Whether it was a parade or some other event, the kids all ended up having a good time on Polk Street. Nobody ever had to worry about crime, murders, burglaries, or any of those things back then. If we could ever have another place like Polk Street, I think this world would be so much better off.

No wonder I can't get any work done ... I can't see through the tears, remembering those wonderful days on Polk Street.

Chapter 14

Ben Discovers Galileo

Did you ever sit down to eat when you're not hungry? Well, it is even harder if you're standing up!

I am sitting at the word processor and I am trying to think about Galileo High School. When you mention Galileo, you think about the telescope, you think of the pendulum, etc. ... Well, my father's first store was called Galileo Market. Do you know that market is still there and successful, three owners later? **But it wasn't to be for my father and his partner at that time, who was a musician in the symphony and marched to a different tune** ... So they broke it up, and my father ended up at Russian Hill with his own market, which is where this book began.

But Galileo High School was another thing ... They don't make high schools like that anymore. We called it "Gal" and I went through grammar school, junior high, high school, university, the War ... and nothing comes close to Gal. Galileo himself was famous for the pendulum, the telescope and stuff like that in Italy. **Galileo could have been even smarter, I guess, but**

he didn't want to show off ... you know how modest Italians are!!! At Galileo High, the *Pendulum* was our newspaper and the *Telescope* was our annual album.

You know that Galileo, when I went there, had no crime rate at all ... I don't ever recall any incidents. I remember it consisted of about 50 percent Italians, 5 percent Chinese, and 50 percent others ... **I can't recall any absentees because we always had that 5 percent extra Italian leeway!**

Galileo High was two blocks away from San Francisco Bay, two blocks away from Ghiradelli Chocolate Factory, two blocks away from Fort Mason, and about four blocks away from Yacht Harbor, one of the most beautiful sites in the entire San Francisco Area. There was more money in Yacht Harbor than in Bank of America in those days.

At Galileo you could smell chocolate all day for free ... A chocoholic would have a ball, I guess. So even the surroundings at Galileo High were great!

My friend's father had a famous pie company that sold pies for as little as 20 cents a pie. They had blackberry, apricot, apple, boysenberry, lemon, custard; you name it and they had it. They used to come around the school and the area, selling these pies. We would always split a pie in half and enjoy it with our lunch. Also, there was a corner store that sold sandwiches for ten cents. I used to have my favorite sandwich with Philadelphia cream cheese, jam of my choice (my choice was apricot), and chopped walnuts. I still make the sandwich of my childhood days at home ... **Somehow, inflation ruined everything but the memories ... but then again, I'm probably inflating the memories.**

Galileo High was only about eight blocks from our store ... In the first three years, I ran back to the store at 12:00 noon. We were on a split system with Lowell High, due to a school shortage at that time, so at noon, we were finished at Gal.

Right before my senior year, I got involved with journalism and sports ... Before I knew it, I was writing for the school paper, the *Pendulum*, and became their sports editor. There were about twenty girls and three boys working on the paper. Of the boys, one guy was in charge of ads, another was the business manager, and I was starting to get into the writing of the paper. My restless attitude soon had me involved in all kinds of changes in journalism and the school album and monthly paper. It was all for the good, as things always stayed the same until I came around — at least that's what my mother used to say!

I had some funny ideas about making the paper funny; that was the funny thing about me ... and it wasn't funny. At that time, feuds were the rage on all the radio shows. Jack Benny and Fred Allen, long before your time, both had radio shows and each would end his show with some caustic remark about the other ... it was fun and so the feuds continued. **I always said there should have been a Pure Feud Law against that sort of stuff!** I had a lot of fun as I started some feuds in our own school paper.

In our school yearbook, we always had to include the required clubs, the senior class pictures of the graduates, and all the other so-called required stuff ... there was hardly any room for change ... but I had ideas of my own and pretty soon, in between the ads I had jokes and candid shots to pep up the album.

Italians were good at sports and many of them brought big fame to Galileo. I do not want to isolate Italians, but I want to tell you why I mention it ... You see, Galileo was fairly close to North Beach, and North Beach was home to many Italians and many, many future athletes ... For example, Hank Luisetti became world-famous when he startled the entire basketball world with his famous "push shot" ... There were guys like Dr. Bobby Brown of the Yankees and later Baseball Commissioner of the American League, who, in one Galileo game, hit four homeruns. The

DiMaggio family made world history ... Joe DiMaggio came to Galileo, talked to the principal, then two hours later went off crab fishing with his father, and that was the end of his Galileo schooling; but his brother Dominic DiMaggio of Red Sox history sat next to me in typing class. Vince DiMaggio also went up to the Big Leagues. My cousin, Frank Lucchesi, became a Big League manager.

Other stars from Galileo were Dino Restelli, "Beans" Marionetti, Nino Tornay, Dario Lodigiani, Marino Pieretti, Walter Williams, Ray Canepa, and Lou Landini. Norm Thompson played for the Colts and Cardinals ... In a chapter like this, I know I am going to forget somebody, so if it is so, please forgive me.

Later, my good friend Lou Micheli, who could remember every detail of sports, would help me on the Hall of Fame Committee ... He was one of the few lightweight all-city basketball champions ... you guys, I hope I don't forget you ... And I will tell you something hardly any high school in America had: we had crew — yes, real live crew in high school. The former crew members come to our reunions and remind us not to forget that crew was alive and doing well in 1937 ... And finally, we had swimmers that made the Olympics, like Patty Elsner, Ann Curtis, Joe Marino, and Reno Rapagnani.

I am sorry to report that James Kearney, the former principal of Galileo High School, Beans Marionetti, and Lou Micheli all died in the year 1995, since this chapter was written. Jim was a former principal of Galileo High that kept this Hall of Fame alive ... Jim loved teaching and sports, and appointed Jack McCaffrey, a Galileo teacher, to head the Galileo Hall of Fame. It was through Jack's talent in putting all the pieces together that we have this wonderful program. There will never be a high school with the records of Galileo High School in sports. **Remember Giuseppe Portaviartecomosichiamo? ... He was one of the big Italian names ... he never made the football team, but he was one of the big names.**

We had dinner last week in a neighborhood place in San Francisco and who should walk in but Grover Klemmer and his wife. Grover was famous in the Olympics as a runner, probably breaking the 880 in 440 time or something like that ... and Grover wasn't even Italian! Grover said the same thing to me about Galileo ... but **I can't remember what the same thing was that he told me about the same thing** ... anyway, Galileo will always be noted for its great athletic stars. **One year we won 17 championships out of 14, and that was pretty hard to do, unless you went to Galileo!** Somehow, they just don't make schools like that anymore!

During my Galileo High School career as sports editor, I was instrumental in the program to enlighten the advertising section with humor.

Chapter 15

Freddy's Famous Sangwiches

You know I almost forgot to tell you about the famous Freddy sandwiches we used to eat ... This old Italian guy had a little store that was only a few blocks from Galileo High School. He had a few items on the shelf, like Italian olive oil, anchovies, and sardines; he also sold "coppa" (poor man's prosciutto); and all kinds of salami, that hung on the wall to dry and get firm. Now, Freddy had been there for years, but I can only tell you about the sandwiches ... Even if you bought all the makings for the sandwiches, you couldn't duplicate them ...don't ask me why! I was a certified, gold-plated Italian boy, and I never came close.

Right now, my mouth is salivating like a hound dog that hasn't had a drink of water all day, just thinking of one of these famous Freddy's sandwiches. When we were kids everyone called them "sangwiches." I can remember saying I wanted a Freddy's sangwich. Now that consisted of a real fresh baked Italian French bread that the grocery stores couldn't buy ... the company he bought the French bread from did not make a bake like that for the regular stores.

Let's go back 50 years or so and pretend we are going to Freddy's Sandwich Shop ... no class involved, wooden boxes that imported goods came out of, customers waiting for their turn to purchase their sangwich ... The bread was about a foot long and it would be sliced in two. You got boiled ham, cheese, salami, and boiled salami. Then you would get mustard on the bottom and mayonnaise on the top. People would buy these sangwiches for picnics, dinner, parties ... and this little Freddy never changed ... You know, I got to know him later in life, after the War, and he was the same guy; he never smiled and life was like the world — serious ... yet he carried on a most profitable business; I'll bet when he died, he must have left a fortune. In relation to Galileo High, many of the kids still go there to get a Freddy sangwich.

A millionaire movie-type of person recently visited San Francisco and some friends of mine took this woman star all over the City. The part she remembers was the Freddy's sandwiches. They took this woman to Fisherman's Wharf, Coit Tower, the S.F. Zoo, North Beach, Chinatown, the two bridges, every sight in S.F., and whatta you know, we're back to Freddy's Sandwiches. Oh well, who said life was simple! If you saw this place, you wouldn't bet five cents on its success. Even Bernard Baruch probably wouldn't be able to figure it out. Well, they had to bring this star back for some sangwiches to take home before she left ... How do you like that?!! Good for Freddy! **I never knew he was so well bread, but he must have ended up with all the dough, because he never spent it ...** He always seemed to have the same clothes on. I will always remember him at the store, never smiling, all serious, and always successful. **Freddy was always ready or not, here I come.** I was told that **Freddy later died at age 102, hopefully not from eating too many of his famous sangwiches!**

Now this vignette came back to me by one of my very best buddies, Walt Biondi. My friend Walt can do anything ... fix watches, fix anything that cannot run, drive like **Hardly Davidson** ... there is no favor too big that he can't do for you. We are what is known as real Itralian relatives ... his mother and my grandmother's cousin was his sister's brother-in-law's nephew ... only a Calabrese can make a statement like that! I always told Walt that when I wrote this book he was going to be in it, so thanks for the vignette, Walt.

P.S. When I went to Galileo High, these sangwiches were only about 30 cents ... after the war they were about 60 cents, and even now they are only about a dollar-fifty ... kind of reminds me of that joke when a **guy asks the storeowner how much one** grapefruit is and the owner says $1.00. Then he asks how much an orange is and the owner says 50 cents. Finally he asks how much a lemon is and he says 25 cents ... The guy says, "Here's a dime ... I stepped on a grape on the way in." ... That is my definition of inflation ...

P.P.S. I know the correct spelling is "Harley" Davidson, but I wanted to make sure you were alert!!!

Chapter 16

Upstairs in the "A"

I forgot to mention that as we got older my parents decided that we needed more room, so they asked a carpenter if he could build a room for my brother and me. In about three weeks, it was all done and Richie and I moved upstairs into what we called the "A" Room or the Aeroplane Room ... It was knotty pine and a great haven for the two of us and all of our friends. The room was great ... it smelled like a boy's room ... the knotty pine aroma. Soon we had about five to ten fellows, rotating, visiting us, so that we could tell each other our plans for the weekend. In those days, we talked mostly about girls ... that was a new subject as we started Galileo High School.

We started going to the "Y" dances. These were held by the Y.M.I. and the Y.L.I. in conjunction with certain hotels in San Francisco. They were great for young people and very well run ... only non-alcoholic beverages for those under 21 — and most of us were under 21. The dances were held at some of the best hotels in the City, such as the Palace or the Fairmont. Nowadays, kids would spend a fortune to go to these places, but we did it with a couple of dollars. The "A" Room was our chance to discuss "personal" subjects. We would discuss all the mistakes we had made during the dances, like just before the dance would end, when we would try to line up our girls and ask to drive them home. Rich and I had the family Buick so we could take two girls home. Other guys had family cars, too, so we would try to go in some type of combination ... I usually liked to go with another fellow, rather than my brother. (You know how brothers are!).

After the dances, if the girls let us take them home, we would usually go to Coffee Dan's or Bunny's Waffle Shop, since they were nearby for all of us.

In the "A" Room there would be deep discussions entailing our "secret" methods, such as "always ask a girl if she has a girlfriend." Most girls knew all of this, and they probably had their own secret ways. Remember, this was all pure, simple, or pure and simple ... we were all trying to do what was safe and sound.

There was never any talk about big sex ... it was all if we could get a few kisses, or smooches, as I always called them. As San Francisco was only 7 miles in any direction, we always tried to go to a good, inexpensive place near the ocean where the girls could tell their parents they went after the dance.

Sometimes, I would get lipstick on my white shirt and in the morning my mother would always act the make-believe part, "How did you get lipstick on your shirt?" I always said, "Ma, you know some girls are short or fat or skinny and you never know which way they are going to move when you're dancing, and whoops, that's how you get lipstick on your shirt." I think Mama always knew, but was happy when I went through this big explanation.

When we got to Bunny's or Coffee Dan's, the fun would start with small jokes or someone spilling something ... something always happened so we would ease the tension.

Then came Monday or Tuesday night, and it would start all over again ... "You should have asked that Shirley, so we could have had two girls that were together," or "When I said this, you should have said that." It was always the same, but different, with all our young ideas thrown in together ... what fun! And all this happened in the "A" Room.

There were never any dirty words or talk ... it was always plain unadulterated kid's talk. But now, we had a place to talk over our various thoughts and dreams ... Plus, my parents would always serve us hot chocolate and cookies, or whatever we wanted, when we walked down this flight of stairs that separated the "kids" from the grown-ups.

Chapter 17

The Song Sheets

A big part of our growing up, when we were in our teens, was the great interest in the "Big Bands." These bands took over teens in school, at the dances, and all over America. Like every craze, the interest was in knowing all the big bands and their songs and music. A popular outgrowth of this demand were the song sheets with all the words of the latest songs.

All of us teens would buy these song sheets and memorize the words of the most popular songs of the times. They sold for ten cents ... what a bargain! There was the Lucky Strike Cigarette Show that played the big 10 or 15 songs, and you never knew which was going to be the winning song of the week until the last song was played.

At that time, bands like Glenn Miller, Harry James, Tommy Dorsey, Horace Heidt, Jimmy Lunceford, Les Brown, Gene Krupa, Ben Bernie, Benny Goodman, and Sammy Kaye dominated the scene. When they were around, the whole world was singing a happy tune all day long. And wherever music was played, singers followed ... soon there was Frank Sinatra and Rudy Vallee, Bing Crosby and Perry

Como. What a legacy we were to enjoy! Little did we know that future generations would cherish the Bands and all their records, even fifty years or more later.

Now, up in the "A" Room, we would memorize those songs, buy the records, and hope that we would see these stars and their music. I was just getting into music and dancing and wanted to improve. You will remember that in my high school period, I was either bashful or not very self-confident, so I was always trying to practice dialogues or patterns.

With the new stars, I picked up a few new lines like, **"I know Frank Sinatra's little brother, 'Not So Hotra,'"** or "Do you know the Don Ameche song? You know, **'I'll be Don Ameche in a Taxi, Honey.'"** When you are seventeen, most guys and gals don't even know how to start a conversation, let alone dance or have fun. Believe me, **I started to think I would be a stand-up comedian, except I hated standing up too long!**

Let me leave you with this thought ... "Good Night, Sweetheart," sung by Bing Crosby, must have been sung a trillion or maybe even a scrillion times while I was in my teenage years.

Rich was seventeen months older, but I was cuter. My mother told me so, and I believed her. She was always right. I was about 4 and Rich was about 6.

Chapter 18

Richie's 17 Months Older than I Am

Rich, or Richie, was older by 17 months and all my life, I never forgot that ... he remained 17 months older all throughout my life. He was better- looking than I was; he was smarter than I was; he was sharper than I was; he was a whiz in mathematics; he drove our little truck at about 12 or 14 years of age because our father, who art in heaven, talked the City into the fact that if something happened to him, no one else could drive to the produce market to get the food with which we made a living.

Now, these were just openers ... Rich was also more coordinated than I was and could play baseball better and football better; he could play the piano and he could do the whole smear better ... BUT ... throughout life, I could do only one thing better (at least, I thought that), and that was talk. Brother, I could talk and talk and talk. My mother used to say, when all else failed, "That's all right, Benny, you're going to be the lawyer in the family." My father used to say, "When Benny gets after you, forget it ... give it to him — it will be easier, better, and cheaper than to argue with him; when he gets something in or on his mind, forget it or we will all suffer."

Rich grew up and was ahead of me by three terms and, by the time I got to Galileo High, I was fourteen and Rich was three terms ahead of me again ... that guy never gave up!

I loved working in the store more than anything. I used to figure out things way, way ahead of time, while Richie always was sort of a dreamer ... he always had a girl or something on his mind. My life was much simpler — all I ever thought about was the store. Nobody, but nobody could "out-store" me; I never tired of the store.

At the store, Richie got all the non-working jobs. I can't remember Richie doing any physical work ... he was always doing more important work — like working the cash register; like opening the store; like closing the store; like driving me to all the orders we had, where I brought the groceries in to the customers while Richie waited in the car and daydreamed.

I remember Rich's first mental girlfriend ... he would say he liked someone, and that became a fascination with him. I remember a girl named Donna who lived near our store and home ... he would walk behind her and her girlfriends, and every day we had to hear how much closer he walked near Donna. He never let us forget Donna.

As I mentioned before, Galileo High School was on a two-school program, so we only went half-day. After school, I couldn't wait to run to the store, about eight running blocks away ... and I did run, to be the first guy back at the store. There I would work on the produce counters and, with no equipment, no refrigeration, no space, no nothing, I did my very best to keep this department pretty. I was constantly adding humor to the store with my stupid signs and ideas.

I remember one vacation my parents took for about a week. I told all the customers to tell our parents of all the fun they had reading the signs I made for our produce department. For example, we had our beets, turnips, and carrots in one stall, so I made a sign like, **"Don't turnip your nose, because you can't beet our carrots,"** or **"We won't carrot all if you try our beets"** ... kid stuff like that, but remember, I was only a kid. Then we had fruit jokes like, **"What a Peach of a Pear this Apricot is"** ... again, only kid stuff, but the customers wished *their* kids had my enthusiasm.

Now, where was Richie during all of this time? He was probably thinking or daydreaming ... that was his cup of tea.

I remember, we used to eat in the back of the store ... it was almost a ritual. My mother would go in the back, where we had the kitchen, and start preparing the dinner. She would make all kinds of vegetables, like Italian string beans with tomatoes chopped up with potatoes and a little bit of pure olive oil; a dish called rape, which were wild greens, par-boiled and then fried in olive oil, garlic, and mild red pepper ... Who could reproduce these dishes?!! Practically nobody. I can think of other things I liked ... dark black figs sliced when they were overripe, with pastry cream on top ... boy, did I like that! ... Which reminds me of something I left out of the book ... One time I got a little fat and a customer said to me, "Hey, Benny, you are getting a little fat." Do you know what my reaction to that was? I ran everywhere — in the store, to Galileo High School, to the delivering of orders — and within two weeks I was perfectly fit with not an ounce to spare ... Gee, now I go on every diet in the world just to lose five pounds! I spend more on books on how to lose weight than the weight I lose ... oh well, life goes on. The back of that store was a glorified restaurant, and don't think the customers didn't appreciate coming back to say hello to the family ... and, oh, by the way, have a little dish of mostaccioli.

As I told you before, while we were eating dinner, my father always used to ask, **"What is the**

**difference between 4,300 and 2,500?" ... that's
what I used to say, "What's the difference?!!"**
That's right, who cares! Rich always knew the
answers. Mama would come from behind where I
was sitting and say the same old thing, "That's all
right, Benny is going to be the lawyer in the family."
It never changed and it went in one ear and out the
other ... Somehow, nothing could make or break me;
I just went right on, like gangbusters ... Benny was
going wherever Benny wanted, and nobody could
defeat him.

As we got into high school, Richie and I and about
six other kids our age started using the Aeroplane
Room for all our talks. We started talking sports, or
school, and then, believe it or not, girls ... Girls? What
was that all about? So we were growing up. The
girls liked Richie better than they liked Benny ... now
this is in Benny's mind, not Richie's ... remember,
**Richie had nothing to do with my life, but he had
a lot to do with how my life turned out.**

I was dark-complected; I thought that was bad ...
I had an inferiority complex about that ... it turns out
it was an asset. But I always kept wishing I could be
like Richie. Richie could dance better than I could
... now, what did Richie have to do with that?
Nothing. All these things I wished I could do better
had nothing to do with Rich, but they all went to

make me strive to be Benny and not Richie. **Freud, where are you now, when I need you to explain all of these things to me?**

I still remember a dance we went to where the girls were figuring out who they wanted to drive with. I didn't even know how to drive, but I heard a girl say, "I'll take the good-looking one." (That wasn't me!) All of those things gave me an inferiority complex ... I never had real confidence. With that in mind, many of my thoughts turned to, "How do I counteract that situation?" Another time, we all were going to the playground to play a big softball game ... I had my mitt all oiled up and ready ... two of the best players were choosing the sides. Rich was taken in the first three or four guys. Where was I picked? I wasn't. I don't blame them ... I wasn't that good anyway. **Baseball isn't the only game in town ... I do other things well. Like what?!!**

Oh well, you didn't have to worry about an inferiority complex in the store ... I could run rings around everyone when it came to waiting on customers or cleaning the store, or coming up with ways to do more business ... now you're talking my language.

Now, we come to the parting of the waves ... **this is where I start my comeback. (Hey, I didn't even**

know I was behind!) When I got involved with
journalism and they appointed me Sports Reporter
for the Galileo paper called the *Pendulum*, this was
right up my alley. In no time, I had columns and
columns of ideas pertaining to journalism. I started
a column called "Benny Sent Me." Then, I started
picking which teams would win the games or which
teams would win the pennants, and all that interest
made me a fairly well-known kid at Gal, as we called
Galileo High in those days. Pretty soon, my mother
and father became aware of their little Benny ... gee,
I was starting to get popular ... **I didn't know where
I was going, but I was going.**

Now, we forgot about Rich ... but he was going to
junior college, and the war rumbles were starting ...
everyone was learning a little bit about Germany. I
started to really like journalism, and was told by my
journalism teacher that I had a flare for writing. As
the war was changing a lot of people's plans, College
of Pacific, to keep business going, started a program
where students from San Francisco could go for two
years to College of Pacific for no tuition or fees. My
teacher reminded me to look into that program, which
I did.

College of Pacific was a beautiful college in
Stockton, California, about 40 miles from San
Francisco. Now this was a rich man's school and

had one of the finest journalism divisions on the West Coast. My mother could not believe it when she heard I was accepted. She was worried about her little Benny, so she made her Richie quit J.C. and go with me to C.O.P., as it was called, so far away from home!

My father had bought our first real good car, a 1936 Buick, and Rich could drive us and bring us back every week with no sweat ... We began going on Sunday afternoon to Stockton and coming home on Friday afternoons to San Francisco.

Our first year at C.O.P. was fun. We had an apartment (student facilities) and I made the beds, I cooked, I cleaned the place, I did whatever needed to be done. I was so excited, I never thought about what Richie did ... but Richie was Richie, and we never knew ... he always seemed to be thinking; what he was thinking, nobody ever knew.

Actually, I have to thank Rich for making me, without him knowing it, into what I am today. I give Rich credit for the brotherly competition that helped me mold myself into my own person, improve my personality, almost finally forget about any inferiority complex, and go on to a productive and certainly a great life.

Graduation Day

This is my High School Graduation Day picture. I was not quite 18. When I was young, this picture never appealed to me. Now that I am older, it looks good. Come to think of it, it looks great. I remember graduation. I took a girl out, gave her a gardenia… everybody gave gardenias in those days; later we went to Coffee Dan's, met a lot of the graduates, and then went to Yacht Harbor, smooched a little, and it was all over. I think the whole Graduation Day was a strain and most of us young guys were glad it was all over. When you get older, you wish you could be young again… wasn't it crazy? This was 1937. What I would give to be 17 and 7/8ths again!!!

Chapter 19

What's Right is Write

I was lost in college ... I mean the studies. My little high school did not prepare me for college ... but I struggled through and started to cope with what I was finding out I didn't know.

It started off with "Bonehead English," which I found out that 90 percent of the students flunked no matter where they came from. I was ushered into a big auditorium at C.O.P. They gave me a Blue Book and a pencil and on the movie screen were instructions for the test. Here I was faced with my choice of what subject I could write about: "Should America Enter the War?"; "The C.I.O. vs. the A.F. of L."; "Strikes"; and so on down the line. I was frozen for about five minutes ... Finally, my store-trained personality came out of me and I wrote like this.

"It was strikes all right and Mike Kelly continues to throw strikes. It was an amazing ball game ... The underdog Lions, pitching with an unknown Mike Kelly, have astounded the baseball world ... Here it was the ninth inning ... Mike Kelly was beginning to look tired ...two men out and the lone run by the Lions

had held up until now. The coach came out to see if Mike could pitch to the one last batter ... Mike asked Coach Russo, 'What do I do, Coach?' and, without hesitation, Russo said, 'Do what you've been doing for over eight innings ... throw strikes.'"

Well, I was recommended to the journalism class and was one of the few male students that passed the "Bonehead English Entrance Exams."

In journalism class, our first subject to write about was our last vacation ... I had never, ever had a vacation in eighteen years. So I wrote about a mythical vacation ... one I dreamed I had ... My article was called "Para-Disla." The teacher brought me up in front of the class, asking where I had copied this story ... And she would see next week ... the topic would be a sports story. Again, I wrote a story like this.

"The game started off with Cigar in the box and Smallpox catching. Corn was in the field and Pancake was at the hot corner ... Glue was at the stick. Glue got a hit and stuck to first. Song made a hit and Glue went to second ... Sawdust filled the bags. The crowd cheered when Spider caught a fly. Soap cleaned the bases ... They took Cigar out of the box and Ice came in ... he kept cool until a ball hit him on the head; then you should have heard Ice Cream! They

lost, but if Door would have pitched, he would have shut them out!"

Oops! Up in front of the class again! ... Where was my source? It was unbelievable ... I was the first freshman ever recommended for the Publications Committee; it had always been reserved for seniors, as a reward for all the work they did for their school. Throughout my life, I never forgot that year in college and, until today, I never fulfilled my dream of writing commercially.

At College of the Pacific I was on my own for the first time
in my life. Besides getting into journalism, I got active
with the female department. I am in the white sport coat...

next shot is me in a tuxedo… bottom shot shows me in a prayer position again…

ALPHA KAPPA PHI

These shots are just a few of my fraternity brothers, to show you how it was at C.O.P.

GINN   HANEY   HEDGES   HELLMAN
McCARTHY   ROSE   SAVELLI   SCANTLEBURY

Chapter 20

The Water Boy

You know something? I must be going crazy. Did you ever hear a guy say, "I don't know any jokes," then he proceeds to tell you 50 new jokes? Well I had a lot of fun at College of Pacific, but I was subdued, whatever that means. I did not have the confidence I had at Galileo High School. I was alone. No brother. He was in the Army. No grocery store; that was 60 miles away. Well, College of the Pacific had one famous coach finishing his career. He was world-famous from the early days of football. He was Amos Alonzo Stagg. A landmark. Well, only because of his fame, a game was to be played in Berkeley - the first time ever that a small school like COP could have ever gotten to play in a big game like this one. Imagine, it was like Galileo High School playing against Notre Dame.

I had gotten a little popular because of my writing an article about the "dink," so they nominated me to be the water boy for this game. The dink was a freshman hat we had to wear, no matter where we went; if caught not wearing it, we would be punished. You know, like clean up the stadium, 20 laps around the track... it was almost an honor to even get punished. Now that I have my senses back, I realize all the things I accomplished or had privy to as a young boy. Remember now, this school was really only for the rich, but through a fluke, the upcoming war, they allowed transfer students from San Francisco for no tuition and no fees. It was a break of a lifetime, and my San Francisco teacher told me that it was a great school for journalism. So now you know how I got to be the water boy for the most famous coach in existence, at that time... Also, the game would be played in Berkeley, California, only 20 miles from my home.

When the time came, I started to realize the importance of everything. Coach Stagg was nearing 80 years of age, the only coach in the United States that age, and here I was going to be the water boy. Now I get a little hazy about what happened, but I must have been a little scared; I don't remember. Now California was favored by about 40 points or "off the boards betting," as the gamblers would say. Up until that time, I had never been in the locker room, where I could hear, "Like win one for the Gipper" or famous Rockne words, but my job was to bring the little tray of water, some towels at every time-out, and when the Ref's whistle blew, for me to get out of the huddle and run back to the sidelines. To get to listen to Coach Amos Alonzo Stagg... that would be a horse of a different color.

The game went at it pretty good and, if I can remember, Cal was only ahead by one touchdown. Soon it was halftime. I ran ahead of the team and was in the locker room. I was in a corner, where no one would even see me. I had never heard a pep talk and coach Amos Alonzo Stagg was going to talk.

Zoom, Zap, Alla Cazam or whatever. Coach Stagg was yelling at his players, encouraging them to do even more, and so on. I practically went in my pants; **I had air-raid spelled backwards, which was diarrhea.** (That didn't really happen...) I will never forget his talk, but I guess with his many years of experience, he knew how to get the boys going.

The boys from little COP College, as we were called, were overwhelmed, but what a fight they put on... according to the papers, you would have thought we won. Little old College of Pacific was praised in all of the papers and many thought that Amos Alonzo Stagg, the father of football, would retire soon after.

Even I, who was only the water boy, was overwhelmed. If ever I were in any sport or business, or even in the War, if I could energize or enthuse people the way that Coach Stagg did on that afternoon in Berkeley before thousands and thousands of fans, I would be the proudest man the world!

CALIFORNIA 20
PACIFIC 0

On the basis of early-season show-
ings, Bay area sports scriveners tagged the Bengals "a junior college
squad." That was before the dog-fight at Berkeley. Showing fine
spirit and determination, the Staggmen held Cal's gorgeous Golden
Bears, Rose Bowl champs, to a respectable 20-0 count. Courageous
line-play with Fullback Mike Martinovich as spearhead of the defense,
forced Bottari, Meek, Chapman, et al, to put out extra steam.
Swagerty and O'Hare were standout forwards. Al Soper matched
the redoubtable Sam Chapman boot for boot, a big factor in holding the B'ars at bay.

THAT THE FROSH WITH "DINKS" ON HEAD, REPENT FOR
HAVING ONCE FORGOT TO WEAR THE "DINK" . . .

AMOS ALONZO STAGG

After completing forty-nine years of
football coaching and six of those at Pacific, Amos Alonzo Stagg is still turning
out gridiron warriors meshed in units of
eleven to battle the best of teams and
come out on the top. As Mr. Stagg looks
forward to his Golden Anniversary of
fifty years of coaching American Football
he may feel justly proud of the work he
has accomplished in building not only
powerful teams but strong character in
men. Stressing high ideals along with his
deceptive and intricate football maneuvers, Mr. Stagg has done much to place
value on football training for the modern
American Youth.

Chapter 21

Follies Night at College of Pacific

College of Pacific was famous nationwide for its music and dancing. One night each year, they put on a show called the Follies. The three sororities and three fraternities put on their own show. I can only remember the names of the three fraternities, but just keep in mind there were three famous national sororities that participated also.

Follies night was approaching and we had nothing ... no money, no talent, no artists, no ideas, nada, zilch ... I was the only one in the fraternity that had ever even done anything in the public eye. They asked me to work out a skit.

Alpha Kappa Phi was poor ... no national funds, no money in the bank account, and no talent. The only thing I could come up with was an Olson & Johnson kind of skit. Here is how it would work ... I would pretend to come up with a real good joke. I tell the guys at the frat, "Here's a real good joke ... **My folks are in the iron and steel business; my mother irons and my father steals.**" Now the guys are supposed to boo. The cue is "Boo! Boo! Boo!" ... Three boos and you're out. The Olson & Johnson part is that stuff begins falling from the ceiling ... rag dolls, toilet paper, stuffed animals, plungers, and you name it, but throw it down on the frat house setting that we had.

It was the night of the show and time for the first act ... one of the sororities has four pianos, with four beautiful girls tap dancing to George Gershwin's "I Got Rhythm" ... What a skit! What artists! What talent! Now, as we were the very last skit, I was sitting right near the front row, because when it was time to go on, we had to go behind stage and set up our skit. Wow! The audience gives a 3-minute ovation for "I Got Rhythm."

The next skit is like Ralph Edwards and it is "This is your life, Amos Alonzo Stagg," the 80-year old world-famous football coach at University of Pacific and football coach there at that time. How are you not going to like that ... especially our own coach! Again, a big round of applause.

This went on and on. Intermission, then it was almost our time ... Suddenly, I began thinking, "How did I ever get to College of Pacific? How did I ever get to this beautiful place in the first place?" Well, it was because of the War ... **I was an exchange student ... I guess they exchanged one of these talented people that paid say $2,500 a semester for me;**

because of the War, I paid nothing ... Anyway, it was our time to go on.

Well, my heart was pounding ... I am sitting with about 20 guys in the fraternity and I start reading from a book. "Hey, gang, here is a real great joke: **My parents are in the iron and steel business ..."** The guys all act disgusted, yelling "Boo! Boo! Boo!" The guys at the ceiling respond with the garbage — toilet paper, books, magazines, balloons, plungers; you name it and it came down!

Now, the next joke ... **"I call my girlfriend my melancholy baby ...she has a head like a melon and a face like a collie."** All the guys show thumbs down and start in with the boos — three good boos and the cue is on; the garbage is coming down ... plenty more, and everybody in this high-class place starts to loosen up and enjoy things.

I remember doing this about five times. Finally, I get up and yell, **"The trouble with you guys is you just don't know a good joke when you hear it!"**

Now, the show simmers down and the judges go into a booth and say they will give us the results in five minutes ... some music goes on ... Finally, they come back and, like they do on a lot of shows, they start with Number 3 ...it goes to the "This is Your

Life" number. Everybody yells and screams ... Then they announce the Number 2 act — the "I Got Rhythm" number with the four pianos and four tap starlets.

Now, a big drum roll and they say, "For their terrific number and unusual talent we award first prize to Alpha Kappa Phi for their Olson and Johnson rendition!" Wow! Here we were ... a bunch of nothings ... none of us had any real talent, no money, no experience, no backgrounds ... standing there on the stage and none of us could say anything. Well, the curtain came down and we started jumping on the stage; then we headed back to the fraternity house, which was right on campus.

When we got back, none of us could even speak. Well, as I said, we had no money, no talent, no skills, but we had Luck and Spirit.

Well, I really had mixed emotions ... the War was hitting everywhere ... I knew I could not continue at College of Pacific ... The exchange was only for two years. I would have to transfer to the University of California, which was free ... no money to continue here for my final two years. I did not say anything, but I knew I could never return to this wonderful school. I had enough memories and vignettes to satisfy a lifetime!

This was my graduation from Junior College. When this picture was taken I already knew I couldn't return to College of the Pacific. I was not at my picture-taking peak. Too bad, because I used to be good looking when I was younger! End of joke.

Here I was, walking down the avenue with a few ex-Galileo High school graduates. I was the middle guy. Imagine those two guys on my sides, not even dressing up to walk with me at the University Of California! Frank Pinaglia is on my right. His father was a big executive at Ghiradelli Chocolate Co., just a few blocks away from Galileo High. The guy peeking over my left shoulder became a big executive and a president of Pacific Gas and Electric. His name was Bart Shackelford. The guy on my left, I can't remember his name, but I know wherever he is, when he sees this picture, he is going to be upset that I couldn't remember his name!!

Chapter 22

College Daze

Rich had already graduated from junior college and soon was drafted, and I had to think about life without Rich around ... with Rich gone, they really needed help at home more than ever. I was still working in the store. I eventually transferred to University of California, where **there were thousands and thousands of kids ... and this was no kidding matter.**

Rich was put in the Signal Corp and was sent to March Field in the L.A. area. I was in Berkeley and I was commuting five days per week. Was I ever lonely!

U.C. was a blur to me. **I really never put anything into U.C. and I never got much out of U.C. Who could concentrate ... the whole world was in flames!** The war was going on hot and heavy ... By the time I was a senior, I was tired from studying, working in the store, and commuting back and forth by train. I would fall asleep in the large classes and was doing badly in school. **My grades were bad, my studies were bad, and the War was bad ... the store, my first love, was bad.** We even had a week where the War Rations Board stopped my father and mother from giving out coffee or meats or sugar without the exact amount of ration coupons. Imagine my parents telling Mrs. Customer that her son could not have coffee or sugar when he was on furlough! They always loaned the customer the item and never counted the exact number of coupons; it always came out in the wash.

I was still working four full days in the store plus a little extra. I still never, ever got paid and I was still doing lousy in school, and, what do you know, it was graduation time! My two last subjects were borderline "C" grades. **(I thought I was going into the Submarine Corps., since my grades were all below "C" level!)**

Well, I think Uncle Sam needed more men in the Service, so I did graduate, but believe me I was pooped ... I had lost a large part of my hair from straining my brain, drinking coffee, and studying in the wee hours of the night ... oh, it was my school and my love for my country and my store that caused all the trouble!!

Graduation Day came and my family all were in the 70,000-seat Memorial Stadium, which was filled to capacity to see the Governor of California give out our diplomas. The percentage of college graduates after the War broke out must have been less than 5 percent ... Who knows, maybe less than 2 percent! For my family, it was a miracle, as I was the first one to ever graduate from college ... to me, it was off to the War, as my induction notices were in the mail within days of graduation. At that time, people all advised me to try to get an Officer's Commission, but they were not about to give me a commission. They said if I had a degree such as an engineering or doctor's degree, I might get some consideration, but without some greatly specialized field, it was not in the cards.

I was about a week away from induction when a friend told me that the Army at the Presidio was short of clerical and/or college-educated men and that if I enlisted, I would practically be guaranteed to be able to stay in San Francisco. Also, I would be considered an enlisted man instead of a draftee; they said that was a big difference, and I believed them. So this was THE BIG ONE. The next part of this book will be devoted to the Big One.

Chapter 22 & 1/2

The War and Treasure Island Didn't Mix

I always asked people, "Why did that darned war have to ruin Treasure Island?" Just when the winds of war come to America, we had the great World's Fair. **It wasn't fair to have a Fair** at the same time, but the 1939-1941 Treasure Island Fair had been planned without a war in mind.

I was at University of California and all my classes were on Monday, Wednesday and Friday. 15 units, no rest, with me working at the grocery store Tuesday, Thursday, Saturday and Sunday. Rich was drafted and I was deferred until graduation, to be June 1941. Things weren't serious at first, and there was leniency in America, as we were not officially in the war. The President, with his leanings towards Churchill and England, would do anything short of war to help the Allies. Well, the Japanese took care of that in short order, and we were in the war for keeps.

In the meantime, down at the ranch... there was a Sally Rand ranch at Treasure Island and again we had mixed emotions. Just prior to the sneak attack, we could go to Treasure Island, by crossing the San Francisco Bridge or by ferry. Remember, I told you how I disliked driving, so I went by going to the Ferry Building, taking the ferry to Treasure Island.

Now remember I was now about 19 or close to 20, my brother had been drafted, and I had to get used to doing more things by myself. Don't forget, there were other guys in our age bracket that were drafted. The whole thing didn't mesh any more. I think my entire mental attitude was changing, but I realize now, after the whole show is over, that I was maturing. What temporarily happened, was the world was waking up to realize that maybe things weren't going to be the same.

What I liked at Treasure Island was what little kids like at Disneyland. All the fun things and the great exhibits are a figment of my imagination now. If I had to take a test, I couldn't tell you what I saw or went through. But I remember the big bands like the Dorsey Brothers, Kay Kyser, Benny Goodman, Clyde McCoy... the whole bunch were there for the public. It really was about the end of the road for the Bank after that... it never returned to the same pitch after the war.

I can remember only what I can remember, and what my mind wants to remember. Anyway, here are the pleasant things I remember. I was a great fan of the San Francisco Seals, the local baseball team.

Lefty O'Doul was Manager and Walter Mails was the Publicity Director. Walter the "Great", as he was called, concocted a terrific event for the S.F. Fair. O'Doul, the manager, was to throw out baseballs from the Big Leagues to Joe Sprinz, who was going to catch baseballs that would be caught right in the Fair grounds, a feat never ever attempted in baseball history. What they never thought of was that the velocity of a ball coming downward was astronomically so powerful, it could kill a person. Within a few attempts at catching a ball, Joe Sprinz broke his jaw and ended his baseball career. In today's world, Joe Sprinz could probably sue and get millions of dollars, but it was all forgotten. In those days of pennies from heaven... no big money was ever given for things like that.

Another memory of the Fair was a guy that came around playing a "toot de ro" or a gazoo. He played all kinds of songs and made it sound so simple and easy to play. I think he could manipulate his mouth so sounds came out great; you thought all you had to do was buy it, practice, and presto, you were a one-man band. We all bought them. The guy had a monologue out of this world that was enjoyable to hear after you were all walked out... And finally, the big event was always the aquacade. Imagine Johnny Weismuller of Tarzan of the Apes fame and the great swimmer, Esther Williams, in a swim show; all I can remember is that both of them became world-famous in Hollywood after the War was over.

One final note... in writing this long after the War, believe it or not, I have blanked out many terrible or sad things or sequences, and no matter how hard I would try or attempt to remember, the good Lord has seen to it that I cannot recall many of the sadder events. I have a bad habit of getting into trouble and many of my friends always claim I only remember the good stuff. You know, **My Silent Partner seems to know what he is doing, so let him make the big decisions and leave the little stuff for guys like you and me.**

Chapter 23

Patriotism

Our family was as patriotic as patriotism could be ... my sister Roberta was selling war bonds; my mother and father were working hard in the store, keeping track of all the food rationing problems; my brother Richie was in the Service; and I was already notified, upon my graduation, that I was to be drafted. Now, how patriotic can we get? I'll tell you how patriotic we can get!

The War brought all kinds of problems because we were not adjusted to war. The U.S. Government was so pure, honest, and good; they were constantly trying to not hurt a soul, and that sometimes brought more trouble than it was worth. Now, because they were going to bring on rationing, they had to announce ahead of time all the items that were going to be rationed — all the items that would be scarce ... How many warnings could they give the scalpers! Now, our family would not be a party to that kind of stuff because we had two boys that were going to help the U.S.A. But let me tell you of the only incident about rationing that embarrassed us a little bit ... not a lot, but a little, because of our purity, and

I mean my mother and father ... we were too young to be embarrassed.

There was to be all kinds of rationing, but the one that the public was mostly concerned with was food. Naturally, you eat three-plus times a day, and even skipping one meal would mean a lot; so food, I think, was number one with most people. Tires, gasoline and a million other things, like nylons and cigarettes, were starting to be in short supply. Importing became almost impossible, so trouble followed trouble.

The rationing for food had different color rationing tickets, or coupons. Meat might be red; coffee might be blue; sugar might be white ... I can't recall the colors, but those three items in a grocery store brought the most problems. Sometimes items like butter were included with the red, and other items, such as chocolate or tea, might be put in with coffee ...so it was all kinds of additional work for the storeowners.

Now, remember what I said about good old U.S.A ... they did not want to hurt anyone, but their announcements made some people rich and some poor ... we were never involved ... but many, many rich people stored up supplies upon any announcements pertaining to rationed items. Now we are getting close to what our little problem was: old customers that had children and almost every family that had somebody in the Service, would ask my mother and father to give them rationed food for which they were short of coupons. My family, who was on a first name basis with 99 percent of our customers, would help the customer; likewise, 99 percent of the customers paid them back the next ration period; so it was all in trust ... my family had nothing to gain by helping the people that asked for it, and they had no experience in this war-time period.

I am not going to make a short story long, and I am not going to make a long story short ... this was the truth ... a government man came in and checked our coupons. Now the agent talks to my parents. Knowing my mother, the water works start, and now he feels like a rat ... so he explains the system to my parents and tells my father to put a sign in the corner of the window and to NOT sell red coupon items for one week. The agent made sure you could hardly see the sign ... so everyone has a good heart!

Now my parents felt terrible. I never told Richie, and I was about to get out of U.C. at Berkeley at the time, so we took it in stride.

Chapter 24

First Alert —
The War Starts with a Bang for Ben

My brother Richie finally went overseas to Europe ... he was in an Air-Warning Battalion. Writing letters home was not his thing ... so I used to pretend I heard from him and pass it all down to the family. I was in San Francisco, believe it or not, and went home and worked all weekend, if I had a pass, and we were an elite group and had many, many passes; the poor guys in combat areas had none. Let me tell you about my first day in the Army ...

We had to assemble at the Warfield Theater, in San Francisco, which was taken over by the U.S. Army for processing applications. Well, I got there and we had about 100 guys waiting for instructions. There might have been one or two college graduates, but all enlistees.

A master sergeant gave us a lecture and a few laughs and pointers to help us relax. He said you should never volunteer for anything in the Army ... **if they say they are looking for music lovers, they'll have you moving pianos, or if they are looking for guys that like gourmet food, they will have**

you on K.P. This guy had us really enjoying ourselves. Then he asked if any of the guys were from San Francisco. I raised my hand and he said, "I will need you to deliver the Form 20's to the Presidio." (The Form 20 becomes your record as an enlisted man all through your career in the Service.) **"Remember what I said in my talk about volunteering? Well, you're it for this trip!"** All the others were transported in a big truck to the Presidio, which had become Officer's Quarters for the Fourth Army.

By the time I headed for the Presidio, it was hours later and, even worse, they gave me a car ticket ... these were used by kids in school to save money on their fare ... What an embarrassing situation that was!

Remember now, we were at war and there was always the risk that the Japanese could bomb S.F. I had to go on the street car, as they did not have busses in San Francisco in those days. I got into the Presidio and it was pitch dark ... there were no lights at night. A guy in a jeep took me to my quarters.

Suddenly, the big sirens are going off and all hell is breaking loose, and a guy is telling me to clang this big bell to get everyone up, that this was a helluva alert ... Guys were coming at me from all angles ... "Get your gas mask, get your gun, get this, get that!"

and I found myself running with all this equipment, talking to the guy running next to me ... I was saying out loud, **"What good am I? ... I don't know how to shoot a gun! What do I need a gas mask for? ... I don't know where I am and it is so dark I can't see! What a mess I'm in, Ollie!"** The guy nearest me says, **"Don't you know a war's going on?!! ... Just keep your pants on!"** Remember now, I was not in any uniform and, actually, I just got off the bus!

Would you believe it ... the end of the alert alarm went off and everyone was so excited and walking pretty fast to the barracks and I heard an officer say, "Who in hell turned in the alarm?" and I said, "I did." (and I did!) ... "Some guy yelled to me, 'Ring the alarm bell' ... so I did what he told me — I rang the bell." The officer looked at me and said, "Go tell the sergeant that you are that guy and you will get a free day pass."

I will never forget the next day, as everything had settled down and I slept on a bunk. I had no one to help me on how to make the bed, etc. ... but anyway, I couldn't sleep all night and, before I knew it, it was 5:45 a.m.

Everyone was yelling to line up outside. I just tried to imitate what the guys were wearing and ran out. A real live sergeant (just like you see in the movies) is calling out, "Right face! Left face!" and all that stuff, and I am three steps behind everybody ... The sergeant said, "Son," as he must have been about 40 and a real Army sergeant ... "Son," he said, "You are all tensed up; just relax." **I relaxed ... and I relaxed all right, as I passed out completely!**

The boys in the barracks razzed me all through our period of 60 days of initial training ...it seems I thought I was going to be an officer quickly, because I was very at ease with the officers and they knew by my Form 20 that I had just graduated from college, so they gave me a lot of responsible work to do.

Remember now, I was only two miles from home and the grocery store. Rich was overseas and food was scarce, so I put in every minute I had at the store. There was no thought about girls or sex ... Believe me, I was starting to get all excited about girls, but never did I think about real sex; it never dawned on me in those days. I thought that was only in marriage. Remember, I told you before, I was a pretty dumb kid, and I was also very naive.

Let's proceed with this small talk about romance, as it will come about sooner or later as I matured ... Remember, I practically never had much time for that subject ... the store, college and the store, and now the War and the store ... You tell me when I had time to devote to that subject! But we will have plenty of time later to go into it ... I am not trying to avoid it, but it will be a lot of fun later, as my innocence or lack of knowledge on this subject stood me in good stead.

Now you got me so excited, I forgot where I was in the story ... Oh, about my stay in the Presidio ... I got to stay there for 17 months ...that was a long time during the War. In the meantime, my brother Richie was in Europe. He had gone to O.T.C. and had become 2nd Lieutenant and we were all excited about that. There were not many armies left in the United States ... **Things were really hot and heavy.** Suddenly rumors were getting out ... the 4th Army might be flown to Europe.

This was a picture of me, showing my parents how to "Present Arms". It was about my fifth week in the army. I was already a corporal. My calculations were that in two years I would be general.

The real reason we were upped in rank was that there is no place in the "Table of Organization" for a private in an army headquarters. It would be two years longer before I became a sergeant!!!

Rich was 17 months ahead of me. It remained that way even during the War. This picture will show that Rich was ahead of me. But remember, I was in an army headquarters and he wasn't, so **he may have been an officer, but I was a gentleman**, even before the movie was made. Rich was a notoriously bad writer. I used to write to my parents and tell them Rich did this and Rich did that. I made it all up. All during the War, I pretended that I received word from Rich, but my mother was right. Rich had the looks and the brains, but he never beat me writing or talking. My mother was right on both counts.

Chapter 25

The Case of the Missing K.P.

About three weeks after being inducted in the Army, I had an unusual experience. You see, going to the Presidio of San Francisco, where there were more officers than enlisted men, we had NO basic training. The Army was known for basic training. It consisted of at least six weeks of hard work, to strengthen you and teach you the fundamentals of war and combat. We did not get basic training. In the desperate need for men that could type or do office work, they bypassed fundamentals that a soldier needed.

Two weeks after being in the Army, I was already a PFC or Private 1st Class. Now, nobody in the basic Army ever got promoted for maybe 3 to 6 months, and even then, it was unusual ... but there was no room on what they called the "cadre" for privates in an Army Headquarters ... so in about a month I was already a Tech 5 or a Corporal ... Gee, I told my parents I figured it all out that in about one year, I was going to be a general! Well, I had a lot to learn. What I didn't learn was very important ... I had no idea and the Army didn't teach me either; they had a war going on. Remember, I had just graduated from

University of California, and it didn't dawn on me that I was talking to majors, captains, and even some generals every day. I wasn't even 22 years of age. An Army Headquarters is as high as they go ... even Patton and Bradley were not generals yet ... they were in the same position that I was ... **I guess, I was going to be a general — General Delivery, I mean!**

After a few months I noticed that there were a lot of officers but not that many enlisted men. I was told that Army Headquarters had plenty of Brass, but nobody to do the physical work. I'll tell you the truth — I did not know how this incident got started, but I was called in by the Master Sergeant and told that because I had not made my bunk properly, I had to do a week of K.P. Kitchen Police was foreign, at that time, compared to office work. Remember now, we had NO women in Army Headquarters at that time ... Also remember, almost no one went to college in those days. 1941 was still in Depression levels ... **I can't remember what I was supposed to remember — remember that!**

So here I was, an inexperienced soldier, an inexperienced man about town, living only a couple of miles from my mother and father's house, so what did I know what was going on?!! I was plainly inexperienced ... So I had no "fear" of officers ... from morning till late, I was in the office and there was no saluting or Army protocol where I was ... it was like working for IBM or a big office. Also, I was in the Corps of Engineers, and they were all mathematical geniuses now in the Army — they were commissioned immediately, to figure out logistics, figures, and mathematical and military problems.

The Army had to train men, and plenty fast ... both officers and enlisted men ... This is why some of my experiences would never have taken place in the real Army. In the real Army, in addition to the six weeks basic training, you got field training, so by then, you were a hardened man ... **I was almost the same as when I got out of college — just a 21-year old kid looking for a job!**

When you are in the Army, they hand you a rifle, you take it apart in the dark, you go to bed with it; it is your friend and your savior in war ... I never had that kind of training. Remember this, so that in the stories I will tell you, you will understand my innocence. The War was going on at an unprecedented level. America was so great and inspiring ... we could produce more food, more arms, more tanks, more airplanes — if we only had more time ... Roosevelt knew this. Churchill wanted us in the War, and that was supplied when Japan struck in Pearl Harbor.

Because we were short on Army privates, **I guess we were expected to do K.P., which stands for Kitchen Police, which stands for peeling potatoes, cleaning pots and pans, and doing kitchen work.** I had NO experience in that either. The incident I got involved in was this ...

When the Master Sergeant in our Headquarters told me I had to do K.P. for not making my bunk properly, I told him that the one thing I always did right was fix my bed and that there was no way I would leave the barracks without checking my position. For starters, I did not know that I could get court-martialed for challenging him like this, or that I had no say in the matter. I told him that if he needed someone to do K.P., he should have just asked me instead of trumping up a fake reason.

His argument was that in the Army you take orders — you don't ask questions. I told him that I would tell them at the court-martial that I was not allowed to say anything, which was un-American. I said that if he had asked me to do it for the good of the Army, I would have been happy to do it. I did not realize at the time how serious my actions were. But again, my stupidity seemed to stun our Master Sergeant. Now, I realize the Master Sergeant was right in 1001 ways. Time passed and I'm sure the K.P. was done by someone else. Nothing happened, although the

Master Sergeant brought it up now and then. Looking back, I must have been a lousy soldier; but my dumb, ignorant manners were forgiven in that I was not trained in real soldier tactics.

What a fool I must have been to challenge the whole Army ... Maybe if I tell a joke, I'll cool off: **A private just inducted in the Army is walking towards the mess hall, when a general comes towards him. He doesn't know yet that he has to salute ... So the General says, "Hey, soldier, don't you see this uniform?" And the private says, "Don't complain — look what they gave me!"**

Anyway, back to the story ...the Master Sergeant reminded me that Stanford University was looking for college graduates for an experimental language Army Specialized Training Program being started in a few weeks. According to this sergeant, I qualified for this program, as I was Italian. Now again, what little brains I had was enough to warn me that, with the turn of political and war events, it was too hot and heavy for me to remain in Army Headquarters as there was talk of relieving us with men that had minor physical problems but were well enough to take over office work. Besides, it was at Stanford University, 30 miles away.

A week or so later, I was told that, in a surprise move, the 4th Army Headquarters was reassigned as the 15th Army and was flown to Europe to join Eisenhower in his crusade. The 4th Army would remain as the 4th Army and be moved to San Antonio, Texas.

To end this vignette (another of my many vignettes), I met this sergeant in a restaurant in San Antonio after V.J. Day. We shook hands and I apologized. We all had a good laugh ... I only wish I knew where this soldier is today, if he is alive, to apologize again to him with all my heart and soul, because he was a true blue Army soldier of the U.S.A.

"The Colorado Rockies"

My first day in Denver, Colorado was spectacular for a guy who had never seen snow. This was a great day. The stairs were the entrance to Case Municipal Golf Course, one of the finest courses in the U.S.A.

Look how young and happy I looked. This picture was my favorite and I sent it to all my friends and relatives during the War.

This was El Jebel Temple, home to the Army during the A.S.T.P. program. It was a Masonic temple that was sacrificed for the sake of our country. It was always sacred to me. Many of my idle moments there were spent thinking about Ali Baba and the Forty Thieves. The temple was filled with many, many rooms, lavish decor, and here we were destroying it every day. I always thought of this lavish place and that darn war that had come into our lives. Who can even imagine how terrible it was in Europe or Japan! Now that the War is over, I hope they have reconstructed El Jebel Temple to how it looked on the first day we saw it in its true beauty.

Chapter 26

Army Specialized Training Program

The war was on all sides of us. There were many breakouts in Europe, Casablanca, Asia, etc., and here I was, still in the United States, at Stanford University in Palo Alto, California. I was waiting to start the new Army Specialized Training Program for foreign languages. After two or three weeks at Stanford, it was finally decided that we were to go to Denver, Colorado to begin our training ... not too bad!!!

We got to Denver and the 300 of us were sent to a former Masonic temple which had been converted during the war emergency. It had a lot of rooms and an auditorium, plus many advantages ... across the road was Case Municipal Golf Course, and the landscapes in Colorado were breathtaking.

The Army Specialized Training Program (ASTP) was designed for the U.S. Government to have men prepared to interview and interrogate captured enemy troops and to communicate with Service people from other countries involved in the war. Being of Italian descent, I was assigned to the Italian unit. They also had Japanese, Hungarian, German, Russian, and a

few other languages. We were to be made officers
— lieutenants — upon graduation from the program.

In about a week, the government changed its plans.
It was told that too much was at risk in having men
attempt intelligence with captured men from the
country that their own family or loved ones came
from ... they might be tempted to take different sides
or make different decisions. So back we went to the
auditorium to find out that we could no longer stay
in the courses involving our native language.
Practically all 300 of us had to switch. I chose French,
as I figured I could use that more than any other
language after the War.

I will say one thing before I go any further ... the
Blitz methods are great. We had three French
teachers — two men and one woman — all real
French. We got into everything ... every day was a
solid blitz; for example, if we were doing "food,"
we would learn every fruit, vegetable, condiment,
utensil, etc. We went to French schools in Denver,
ate with French people, talked and danced with
French people. Since we were going to be involved
with foreign prisoners, all language levels had to be
considered — high class, middle class, low class.
We had to learn all the swear words, all the sex words
... hey, it was really a blitz all right! We were
supposed to talk the language from morning till night.

It was really intense and enjoyable, and we were going like gangbusters.

But, like any government project, whenever things get too familiar, all the "deals" start, and the government is taken advantage of. For example, at first we were eating great food for war conditions, but soon the caterers started lowering our food quality. One day one of the guys told me the meat was horse meat. He said, "Can't you tell? The fat around the meat is all yellow." Gee, within five seconds I wasn't hungry anymore. Each day of the program brought new changes like that.

Pretty soon, we started to eat across the road in the little coffee shop at the Golf Club. The privates were now making $50.00 per month and the corporals were getting $66.00. Remember how I told you money and I don't get along? Well, I was always lending or treating, so my $66.00 quickly went down the tubes.

Thinking back, how lucky we were! Think of the guys in the battlefields! I was writing to one of my pals that was fighting on an island against the Japanese ... and me — **you know me — if you look in the dictionary under "dumb," or " naive," or "stupid," or "wake up, pal — there's a war going on!" you'll find my picture.** This guy, John, was

risking his life 1,000 times a day, and here I wrote to
him about being next to the golf course and going to
see French girls and eating good food. Wake up,
Benny — your picture must be a lesson in stupidity!
Now, I feel like ten cents. Why didn't I realize how
lucky I was? ... Well, I was there, but I did not have
any pull; I did not cheat; I did not pull any plugs to
get there. If you ever finish this book, you will realize
what I said in the beginning ... I had dumb, innocent,
stupid luck. It was a streak you would not believe.

I had made a vow to myself that I would try to
read four books every two weeks. Well, I did that
during the 42 months I was in the Service. Also, I
had started sort of a diary about Army life ... I thought
maybe some day when this war was over, I could
write a book ... I had called it "Army Daze."

Suddenly, one morning on the bulletin board I saw
that a Mr. Bob Anino was attempting to produce an
Army play called "Army Days." Little did I know
he was a professor at Lowell High School in San
Francisco. He was in the German section. I met
with him and showed him my notes for "Army Daze."
What a great guy he was, and he had personality
coming out of him in all directions, but was a very
modest guy — not like the guy he was talking to.
Bob said to me, "Why don't you come to see us
practice? Maybe you would want to be in the show."

I told him that was not my cup of tea, as I would get too nervous.

Well, I had forgotten about this and one day, after we found out about the "horse meat," three of us guys decided we would go to an Italian restaurant in Denver. We had a big Italian dinner — a 12-inch steak and all the trimmings, plus dessert — for 99 cents! Well, I don't usually drink except maybe one drink with company, but that night I had two Manhattans. Anyway, I felt those two strong drinks, and as we got off the bus and walked towards the Masonic temple, I could hear piano music and a lot of noise. Suddenly, I remembered Bob and his invitation to me to watch them rehearse. Well, we walk in and Bob gives me the royal treatment. Now, Bob plays the piano like Carmen Cavallero (a star at that time). We start to watch and it is interesting and it is sort of like Hollywood — a lot of fun to watch.

He calls for a break and plays a couple of songs from the play ... hey, terrific — I am impressed. So he keeps telling me I would be terrific as one of the stars in the show, John Stettin, or some name like that. Remember, I had those two Manhattans and I laughed at everything. So Bob, the school professor, starts rehearsing and he says, "Hey, Ben ... stand over there," and he kind of tells me what to do. No matter what I do, he keeps saying, "Terrific!" He bawls this John out and says, "Why can't you do it like Ben is doing?" Hey, I didn't even know what I was doing! He makes me promise to just come in and watch practice, as he is going to use some of my jokes in the show ... now, that woke me up big! ... Well, after a few weeks he talks me into being John.

We heard that some big shots were going to be there on opening day. They had also invited a school to the opening show; I didn't know at the time that it was an eighth grade grammar school class.

The show starts and no laughs, no action, no applause. Well, I had forgotten that these kids only knew stuff like Jerry Lewis or Abbott & Costello would do. Once I found that out, I kind of hammered up John's part and all the kids laughed and laughed at that stuff.

There was only one big Broadway show to see at that time, and that was the popular "This is the Army, Mr. Jones." So when they said some generals were coming to "rate" the show, God knows what that meant ... but the show went on. I never, ever figured the show out, but who cares when you get laughs and enjoyment! I never did figure out either if I was any good, but after the show all the baloney starts like, "They are talking about going on tour," "They want three more night shows," etc. Little did I realize that the government was getting close to breaking up the ASTP program, and that was next on the agenda.

It was ironic, because after the war I bought a home in a new section of San Francisco and Bob ended up as a vice-principal at the very school that my children later attended in the neighborhood ... that's show business for you! My friend Bob was instrumental in a lot of sports programs, created "yells" that are still being used, and was just as creative as he was in the ASTP program.

The Army Specialized Training Program

When the United States Government decided to start the "Army Specialized Training Program," we were midway into the War. I guess the Pentagon felt we were unprepared for any surrenders by the opposition, so they created ASTP, a unit they thought could do the job.

The ASTP, as we were called, were going to interrogate with soldiers trained by the War Department . The government was looking for soldiers to train for Italian, German, French, Japanese, Polish, Russian, and other languages that were involved in the war effort.

The government never expected the backlash the program brought to the country. Wives, widows, mothers all wrote to the Pentagon and complained that their husbands, sons, etc. were fighting in combat, while we were enjoying a nice life, learning foreign languages. To pacify everyone the government cancelled their programs and to satisfy the public, all of us in the ASTP were sent to combat units. The picture shows all of us in the program before it was cancelled. See if you can find me in the picture?

"It's A Great Life"

During our training in the Army Specialized Training Program, we were allowed certain hours of leisure. During the day, we studied in a blitz method. It was great. The Army was always thinking of ways to keep the soldiers sharp and the Army enjoyed shows put on, that even the public could see, that would keep the American image bright and with hope.

I had been writing in my spare time about my life in the Army with a book I had named as "Army Daze". In Denver, Colorado it got very cold in the winter and we were indoors most of the evenings. I was surprised to find they were having tryouts for a play called "Army Daze," which was later changed to "It's A Great Life." If you see clearly, I am first on the left of the soldier ready to come down to center of the stage. We had quite a few Air Force generals and high ranking officers review the play. But Irving Berlin came out with "It's A Great Life In The Army" to standing room only. The story of this picture will give you the details.

Chapter 27

Sister Roberta

My sister was born in 1933. **She is not a nun, even though I called her Sister Roberta. I always called my sister Roberta because that is her name, "nun the less"** ... Anyway, one day Papa came into our bedroom to tell Rich and me we had a little sister. I had no idea how babies were born or anything about childhood. Remember, this was the Depression, but this news was news to me — it wasn't depressing. **(De pressing was done by de tailor).** I did remember the kids in Spring Valley Grammar School, where I must have been in seventh or eighth grade, saying that they knew how babies were born. I had no idea at that time ... and it must be embarrassing, or why were they talking funny about it?

But Roberta, or "Bert," was one pretty baby. I don't know why I took over with Bert, but I did. I used to take her down one block to Larkin Street, which was a level street, and buggy her around until I met someone who would ask me whose kid that new kid on the block was.

I had no idea if this was a "sissy" thing, but I never thought about it. I just liked watching her grow up.

Remember, my mother was very important at the store, because she knew all the female customers. I was expendable for an hour or two each day, and Mama liked me to watch Bert for her and give her a break from having the baby straight through the day.

Now, I am not clear about Bert between that time and when I was in the Service, but something that happened then is still in my memory bank ... At that time "Snow White and the Seven Dwarfs" was the hottest movie, and all sorts of Snow White stuff was popular. Walt Disney's firm had girls' dresses for Christmas. Well, I found a dress for Bert that was so cute, it took half my pay to get it. Today if you have a dress like that, it is worth a fortune to collectors ... I told Bert that, and do you know what her answer was? ... "I still have it; I have saved it for my grandchildren." How about that?!!

Anyway, some time after I bought the Snow White dress, I found out that someone had stolen my pocketbook. I was stationed in Denver at that time.

I can't remember if I told you somewhere in this book that **I didn't like money and money didn't like me.** I will also tell you that all my little group of friends borrowed from me, and I treated them to all the shows, etc., as they would go broke every month, since they could not hold on to their money.

When my wallet was stolen, I asked if they could lend me a few bucks until the next pay day; they all had different excuses why they could not help me. I was forced to wire home for money. I also told you in earlier chapters that money was never an issue in our family ... I asked for $50 and my parents wired back $100. This was the first time in 23 years I had ever asked for money. Now, I was devastated that someone in our group had actually stolen money; I actually did not believe anything like that could happen. Who would want to steal someone else's money? Almost all the guys I was with in this Army Specialized Training Program were privates, as the program was designed for educated people that could be used for interpreting foreign languages in the War.

Benny, you are so dumb ... wake up!! Benny, when are you going to grow up? They had better inform you that your childhood days are over! I just want you readers to know, I am not just making this up to show you how cute I was or am ... Innocence is bliss, but I had to grow up sometime!! (**... I know they stole one of the Three Little Pigs because I saw the Disney cartoon, but I thought they found who did it because one of the pigs squealed.**)

Now let's get back to Bert ... she was growing up and in Catholic school with her girlfriends. Sister Bert didn't become a nun; I guess **she would have nun of**

that. If Bing Crosby, in his portrayal of a Catholic priest, had made "Going My Way" a different way, she might have been interested ... Only kidding, Bert ... **You could have been a nun, but you didn't want to change your habit ...**

But let's get back to Roberta. You know, she treated me just like a brother ... (Come to think of it, I *was* her brother!) Anyway, Roberta took care of Mom and Dad while Rich and I had gone to war. When I got back, Roberta was quite grown and was starting Catholic high school. She has remained a beautiful girl. When the big War was over, we all were happy to be happy again. It was all in the family.

There was a time during the war when I wanted to buy a "Snow White" dress for Roberta for Christmas. My wallet had been stolen. None of my buddies had any money to spare. My parents came to my rescue. I sent a Walt Disney "Snow White" dress home.

Later in life, I mentioned to "Bert," "Too bad you didn't save your Snow White dress. It would be worth a fortune." She remarked, "I still have that dress in a hope chest." She was saving it for her grandchildren.

Chapter 28

V-E Day, or Halfway Home

By reading this book, you may have gotten the idea that no matter what Benny does, it turns out that he is the hero or that he is constantly lucky or that the good Lord is taking care of him ... well, that might be so, but I had my share of lousy luck too.

For example, on V-E Day, three guys and I got two rooms reserved for the big celebration. We were going to go to a big dance and meet all kinds of girls that were so glad we were winning the War. We got into the famous Brown Palace, the finest hotel in Denver. Boy, we were all set! Somehow none of us connected ... no glamorous women, no great celebration. The two other guys that had a room got into a big argument ...maybe they had too much to drink; I can't tell you because I don't know and I didn't want to get involved. I still had my buddy, Harry.

Now, Harry kept talking about his girlfriend; she was coming from Boston, so he had promised to show her the Colorado area, especially the tour of the Grand Canyon. Well, Harry and I ate dinner together on V-E night, but he was not too good-looking a fellow, if you didn't know him, so he didn't attract too many girls. I was neutral, so I might get better results ... I hadn't tried to get attached, as I always said I wanted to go home to San Francisco and raise a family there; I never ever wanted to make believe the girl I was going with was it.

That reminds me of a dance I went to in which the girl I was dancing with told me that if I went steady with her, she would give me anything I wanted; I told her she was crazy. I went into my personal feelings on this subject and said that would work with most GI's, but I always let things happen without promising the world.

Well, back to V-E night in Denver, Colorado. Harry kept talking about his girlfriend, and I kept looking at all of the tables to see who was without a male companion and things like that, pretending I was really absorbed by Harry's conversation about his girlfriend. I told Harry to rent the car and we would take the trip to the Grand Canyon, even though one thing I don't like is heights. I will get to the Grand Canyon in a few paragraphs, but right now, here we are in the Grand Ballroom of the Brown Palace and have no connections. Harry was glad to have a buddy for his coming event and wasn't even looking around the hall ... The affair was really to celebrate us winning half of the war ... but you know

men — you not only want to win the war, you want to win it with a girl!

War ... That was really what it was all about, but at the time, it would have been nice to be with a girl on that night. Eventually, we left the Brown Palace and went to another sponsored dance, right near where we had to get the bus to our Headquarters, which was in the made-over Masonic Temple. Harry and I went, but he left early and I remained until the end of the dance. Still no connections, and I started to get sad ... real sad. I found out there were no busses to the Temple, so I started to walk towards the Temple and guess what ... it starts snowing! Talk about tears! Here I was almost lost, no girlfriend, two o'clock in the morning, and I'm alone ... There is one thing I'm not good at, and that is being alone ... then the water works start. I started to cry, and I cried and cried, and said I would never let myself get into this kind of situation again. It was really the only time of the entire War that I felt all alone. I had plenty of time to think of how stupid I was not to stay at the Brown Palace, or to want to go to another dance or whatever I had done to get into this lonely situation. Now, I had three or four girlfriends in Denver ... somehow they were all German, and here we were fighting the Germans, but I guess I liked almost the opposite of an Italian-type girl. (I never really thought about this until now.) ... Well, let's forget about V-E Day. We were halfway home and it was good news for all Americans.

Now we have to talk about Harry's girlfriend. She shows up and not bad — a nice-looking girl. This made me think about how dumb we were; Harry was a nice person ... he didn't need any other girlfriends, and I don't blame him. I was the guy going in the wrong direction ... but remember now, I was already committed to a type of life I wanted and also to the kind of work I wanted to do for the rest of my life. I felt sorry for the people that could not figure out what they wanted to do when the War ended. (I purposely am not telling you what I was going to do, as that will all be in the next book. You will like it. Nothing will be as big as WWII or the Big One, but this next thing I do will surprise a lot of my readers. My next book will be called "I Went Broke in the Boom." Please think about it.)

Now I do remember the name of the girl I took to the Grand Canyon trip in Colorado — it was Gerry. It was so cold, but Harry was driving in the front and smoking his pipe and showing his girlfriend all of the beautiful sights — they were breathtaking ... You have never visited a sight that God created so beautifully. Now, as I mentioned before, another stupid fault of mine is that I can't stand heights. Yes, I can't stand heights and we are up over 10,000 feet!

Harry was another guy that kept telling me he liked the way I talked. I was starting to think my mother was right, because she liked the way I talked. **Oh, I could talk all right, but not right now!** Harry gets out at those locations which are marked for the public and I am still in the back seat with Gerry and two blankets. Finally I get out to observe the beauty but it was cold and I was scared to death of the height ... This is another reason why I made a lousy soldier ... suppose I had been on that trip which General Patton had taken with the Seventh Army — would I have survived? I don't think so. It seems the things you don't like usually don't happen ... the trip we had was great. Harry and his girlfriend really enjoyed our company and we enjoyed theirs ... but now that it is so many years later, I appreciate what a nice person Harry was and what an unappreciative guy I was, but this is all in retrospect.

So that was my V-E Day and my trip to the Grand Canyon — two great events in my life. You know, Denver is called the Mile High City, and I did not realize how the high altitude affects you ... I can imagine now that is why Denver's football and baseball teams will surprise a lot of rival teams, as they are more acclimated than the visiting teams, so they have that advantage.

Now that I have given Denver and my stay with the Army Specialized Training Program its just due, I will close with this thought ... Denver was estimated to be a future great city in the world and the current prognostications are that it is one of the four cities to be nominated for this award.

It was Harry and me for 17 months as we became friends in our Army Specialized Training Program in Denver, Colorado. Harry was in the Hungarian group and I was in the French group. We enjoyed going in to town, which was Denver. In Denver you could eat a dinner consisting of the biggest steak imaginable, soup, cold cuts, salad, dessert... all for 99 cents. Harry was the guy that made me go on that trip to the Grand Canyon.

Chapter 29

B.V.D. Underaware

When you were in the Army it was compulsory for you to see Army films regarding venereal diseases. With the millions of Army people, outbreaks like that could practically ruin a company, a division, a regiment, and so on down the line. Movies were shown on a regular schedule and all enlisted men were required to view them.

The movies were designed to scare the men badly. They contained the sort of stuff that would nauseate them and really make them conscious of the problems the government faced with any outbreak of disease among such large numbers of Service people. When those films were shown, I would close my eyes and not look at these gory pictures.

As I mentioned earlier, I had NO experience in this sort of thing ... Remember, right after high school I had gone to college and spent all my extra time in the store. My first 17 months of service were confined to San Francisco. My next year or so involved ASTP programs regarding foreign languages in Colorado.

The War had gone on world-wide for three years, plus all the earlier years involving Germany and the world ... people were fed up with WAR. They were writing letters to Congress, stating that their boys or husbands had been overseas, injured, and returned back to duty and these kids (the ASTP boys) were still around. Suddenly, the program was shelved and, almost as if in punishment, the Army sent us all to the worst areas, the worst divisions, etc.

Now imagine me, not ever experienced in real combat, being sent to the 1252nd Combat Engineers as a corporal ... I had about 27 months of non-war training and now I was in a combat division. What a revolting situation that was, Ollie!

Determined to make the best of things, I decided I would not go into town for fun; I would not waste my time on non-war thinking. I decided I would go to what is known as the Day Room to read some books on war. The Day Room was a room where they had ping-pong tables, pool tables, and stuff for a guy to relax. We had field manuals called FM's in the room. I had to grab the simplest ones, as I was starting all over again ... the first book I grabbed was simple Army commands. There I was in the Day Room with my field manual. Everyone had gone into town for fun and here I was the only one there.

I forgot to tell you, this 1252nd Combat unit was just being formed and it was going to be one of the toughest John-Wayne-type of units ... so they were recruiting guys that had been in the Army stockade, men that had gone AWOL and had been recaptured, guys with the worst Army records PLUS, for public view, the ASTP boys were being accumulated for this unit. I worried for the first time in my Army career that the show was over ... in the end, I would get mine ...

But as my innocent dumb luck continued, an officer of the day walked in to check the Day Room. I was holding the book, walking up and down, saying, "To the rear, march; right face; left face; to the rear, march."

Suddenly, I see this officer laughing away. Right away I saluted him. He tells me, "You don't salute in the Day Room," and asks me, "Who in the hell are you, and why all this practice if you are a corporal? What's your name?" I tell him and he says to me, "If you don't say anything about it and stay in this unit, I will make you a first sergeant within a week or two ... I like your attitude," he told me, "and you can be in the field office with me."

Come Monday morning, at roll call, my name is called out to report to 5th Army Headquarters. Gee, this was unusual and I kept thinking, "I wonder what they want me for," as I spent my first week shoveling dirt from one hole to another, just to get hardened up for what I would face in the coming weeks.

Monday arrives, and I have to go to 5th Army Headquarters. They ask me questions about my experience at 4th Army Headquarters in San Francisco and I tell them everything. The Major says to me, "I am going to give you a few weeks in my office to straighten out the entire situation at 5th." The office paper work was in such a turmoil it took a few days just to sort out what I was intending to do to put everything in order; then suddenly I see a report requesting any men with a specialization number of 355 to report IMMEDIATELY to 4th Army Headquarters in San Antonio, Texas. I showed this to the Major and he said, "Gee, I finally get a guy who knows office work and I lose him within a week!"

Soon, I was off to San Antonio, back into the same Army headquarters I had started with in San Francisco. Believe it or not, I was back with the original army; as Roy Rogers would say, **I was back in the saddle again** and out of combat duty. I felt I could do more for the war effort, doing what I thought was important work that most military people couldn't do ...

Oh, one last story about my experiences with the 1252nd Combat Engineer Group was a dance I went to for the first time ever ... At Camp Swift, I never had been with combat troops, so I was totally unprepared for how they operated the dances. Now, this was just a few days before my experience in the Day Room. I had made a few friends that had arrived for duty, just the same as I had. One guy named Vince took a liking to me and showed me how to use a rifle and how to face combat life if it came to that; he was a master sergeant on his second tour around with combat troops. Vince did not want to go to the dance ... so off I went in a truck with some other guys.

We got to the dance and I started to dance with a beautiful girl — real beautiful — and, I must say, I was shaping up as a fairly nice-looking soldier ... I could tan in just a few days, as I had an olive complexion and I had a beautiful tan. I was all showered up and in nice immaculate condition. This girl commented on my looks and my tan. Just then, a whistle blew and everyone changed partners. "How do you like that!" I asked a guy on the sidelines, "What happened?" He explained that many times there are too many guys for the number of girls, so they blow a whistle and you change partners.

A little while later the whistle blows and I tag the guy dancing with this beautiful girl. Now I am back in business and we are getting along great ... then the whistle blows and I am tagged. This time the girl intervenes and tells the guy, "Gee, can't you let me finish dancing with my husband!" Wow, I had a lot to learn! Anyway, I finish up getting acquainted with this girl and she gives me her address and phone number and tells me to call her over the weekend. I could hardly wait to tell Vince in the barracks about my good luck! And he didn't want to come to the dance! I ask the girl if maybe we could walk over to where the bus is, thinking maybe I could get a few smooches, but the girl won't even give me half a kiss. I try and try and pretty soon I could hear the end of the music from where I was.

As I told you, **when it came to actual experience, I was a babe in the woods** ... I was still to kiss this girl. Finally, I grab her and give her my best kiss, and then another one. Then, she said, "I'll see you over the weekend. Call me up." I figured she could fix Vince up; I was always the same ... I didn't like to do things by myself, as I really had no experience.

O.K., now I get to the barracks and Vince is talking to some of the guys and I tell him, "Wait until I tell you what happened to me! I met this girl," etc., etc., and then I told Vince about this girl who wouldn't let me kiss her and I finally forced her to kiss me and the whole bit ... and Vince says, "Holy smoke, Ben! She might have been like some of those prostitutes that go around camps and give all the troops diseases ... **it could even be enemy tactics!** That's all you need!" Wow, I could see my parents and all my friends in San Francisco and what they would think if I had a communicable disease! So Vince says, "Do you have anything in your foot locker that can kill the germs?" I said my mother had sent me some Italian salami and I had some Ghiradelli chocolate ... (now Ghiradelli chocolate was simply unavailable at any price). So Vince says, "Let's eat some of that and maybe we can kill the germs." So that's what we did — we ate the whole thing!

When it was all over, Vince told me it was all a big joke to get me to get the Italian salami and Ghiradelli chocolate out of my foot locker ... we laughed and I made believe I knew it all the time — which, of course, I didn't ... Oh well, sometimes it doesn't pay to know too much!

Chapter 30

I Remember It Well

For the life of me, I can't remember how I got to Louisiana, but I did ... it happened, and they were the only maneuvers I ever experienced. I think it took place when we were released from Army Specialized Training and sent to a 5th Army Division in Texas. Well, I was like a hick with no experience, as I still secretly could not shoot a gun, could not do what was to be expected of me, and had no military experience in combat affairs ... Ah, I remember it well ... all because of a Sergeant Hansen, from the old Army, who took a liking to me and was grooming me as his protege to becoming a real live soldier. Sgt. Hansen was about 40 years of age and had already been sent back for the second time and was more or less rehabilitating in America.

Somehow, I guess my innocence attracts older soldiers to me, as they always seem to want to help me in my time of need. Well, this Sergeant Hansen kept telling me that in maneuvers you have to make sure you always know where you are, in case you are lost or captured and, for some reason or other, you must always carry a compass. **Now, a compass, at that time, was like this word processor is for**

me now ... I am lost with it and it never does the same thing twice for me. So here is Sgt. Hansen taking out his compass and telling me Northeast by North, and Northeast by East, or whatever ... It was all Greek to me, but I kept listening to him. I could figure out, no matter where I turned, I was always facing north.

This really made me feel stupid. You know that old joke, and it fits me ... **"A guy says to me, 'Didn't you go to school, stupid?' ... 'Yeah, and I came out stupid, too.'"**

I always pretended I was starting to catch on, but I confess, I didn't catch on ... but I never thought anything would ever come of it, and I used to thank Sgt. Hansen for his help and I told him I was starting to understand about the compass. He always told me to get a back azimuth and start from there ... I still don't know what a back azimuth is, but I am going to look it up, right after I finish this story.

Well, we got to Louisiana and the first night it was so cold you could not sleep ... you know how they tell certain jokes — they will start out, "It was so cold ..." and then comes the joke ... Well, it was so cold where we were on these maneuvers, we had a shift of nuts like me getting wood and throwing it in the fire all night to keep us from freezing. I kept saying to our buddies, "We're here because there is a war going on, but why are these people from Louisiana here?" It was unbearable, but maybe any place outside of California has cold periods ... I kept telling the gang that story over and over ... "We're here because a war is going on, but what excuse do the people in Louisiana have?" Here is another of those things I told you ... as a much older person, and now much more intelligent than I was then, I am sorry to criticize; however, I still can't believe people in Louisiana live there on purpose ... only kidding!

Well, the big event was going to take place and I had to be ready with my compass and my back azimuth instructions. All of a sudden, everyone is yelling that the maneuvers are on ... and here I am, walking down the road with my rifle, my canteen, my gas mask, my pack, and everything, including my compass, when some guys capture me, or whatever they do, and tell me to get into this jeep and they will bring me back to the capture zone ... Gee, and I was just getting started too! I remember it well, as Maurice Chevalier would have said. Oh well, I did not get to use my compass. They brought me back to the "captured zone" and I must have been the first guy captured. They gave me hot coffee and donuts ... I still remember those donuts, as they were the size of three donuts in today's stores. Well, these practice maneuvers went on all night, and by morning they were called off.

I kept waiting for Sgt. Hansen to show up ... but no one knew where he was or had seen him. The next day he was not in our barracks and I kept asking, but no one had seen him. **On the third day of September, three mocking birds** ... no that's not it ... but my good friend shows up — all tired out, needing a shave and a haircut, and haggard, sad and lonely-looking. He evidently had gotten lost in the wilderness of the Louisiana bayous, or whatever they are called, and just couldn't figure out where he was. **I wasn't about to ask Sgt. Hansen if he used his compass or tell him that he should have gotten a back azimuth!**

I never mentioned this incident and we were always friends ... we parted and it comes back to me now ... this was just when I was with the 1252nd Engineers Combat Division, and it was only for a couple of weeks, before the 5th Army Division sent me back to the 4th Army Headquarters in San Antonio, where **I was outstanding. Yes, I was out standing in the rain when they captured me and returned me to my senses ... I REMEMBER IT WELL!**

Chapter 31

Let's Play Dominoes

I remember San Antonio for a lot of reasons ...
What a great place to be — I imagine both to visit
and to live there. The weather is perfectly balanced;
you do have a hot summer, but it's not so hot that
you don't want to be there. The surrounding areas
are beautiful.

I was in the Army, but I still had my individual
way of thinking and enjoyed the same things I always
had, because I had not seen actual war ... So I want
to apologize ahead of time, as sometimes it looks
like I couldn't care less about everybody else or about
the War.

Well, an Army buddy I had in San Francisco was
going with this girl and he was now going overseas.
He told me to call his girlfriend in San Antonio. So
I did. She responded and asked me to have dinner
with her and her family.

The girl told me how to get to her place ... take
the bus and get off at a certain spot. While riding on
the bus I noticed all the watermelon stands ... every
other block. Wow, if you loved watermelon like I

did, it was great. You could sit down, rest, have a cigarette ... Incidentally, the percentage of smokers in the Army must have been 90%, at least. Still, I couldn't get that war feeling.

I got there around 6:00 p.m. Her mother opened the door and greeted me and, after showing me the house, asked if I liked to play dominoes ... I said I did, and she replied, "Let's play dominoes!" Now, let's talk turkey; **the average GI, just as soon as you said he was able to take off, he went to a bar, he went to a house of prostitution, he went to a show, he went berserk ... you name it, he did it. NOBODY played dominoes!**

Before we started, the father wanted to show me their home. He had a room filled with sugar, one with coffee, and plenty of dried hams, bacon, and corned beef to go for 20 years. He showed me the sugar ... about fifty 100-pound sacks. **He told me he was glad he got his share before the hoarders got to all the rationed goods!**

It seemed the government always made the fatal error of telling everyone in advance what they had to do to protect the nation ... that is why every item that became short was because people bought millions more than they could ever use, just to "be prepared" in the event of a shortage. By that time the prices would be sky high and you could never get the items anyway.

Before I went to enlist, when I was still helping my mom and dad in the grocery store, I was selling all kinds of foods that I knew would get scarce. For example, I sold 5 cases of tapioca ... we never sold even one case a year, but when I mentioned it came from Singapore, everybody bought it.

Well, to continue the story about the dominoes ... the mother and I stood against the girl and her father ... we played about three games and the mother and I won them all. Now, I had not played for years, **but that night meant more to me than all the tea in China. Why? Because it had nothing to do with that darn War!**

But the girl wanted to get out of the house for three reasons ... one, she wanted a cigarette (which, I appreciated, for her mother's sake, she did not want to do in the house. At that time, I smoked, too.) The second reason was she wanted to take me to this German country dance they had twice a week. Thirdly, I guess she wanted to smooch a little and have a drink ... **We did both of those three things!** Hey, remember how I told you how dumb I was ... stupid, naive, all those things? Well, maybe I was stupid, but I wasn't dumb! See, but I did not have that war anxiety ...

I remember all of us that perspired took salt tablets and at evening time you could see the white circle of salt on the uniforms of the GI's. On the way back that night, I was wondering if I would remember all these little things ... I might never, ever, ever come back to this place ... which, so far has been true. When I got back to Fort Sam Houston that night, I said to myself, "I had a good time; I really had a good time" (a la Ernest Borgnine).

I went out with this girl many times and I always respected her parents; but I got the biggest kick out of her mother, who made these lines famous: LET'S PLAY DOMINOES.

I almost left out the ending ... this girl somehow felt, because her parents had a car which she would get to use when we went out, that the car was the reason I went with her. She mentioned that to me ... and I told her how much I would miss the car. **I actually missed her mother more than I missed the girl** (only kidding)! But I did not call her for about a week after that. The mother called and told me that her daughter was crying and smoking and drinking again and asked me to call her up. Well, I still did not do that. Soon I got a letter in a black envelope, saying how miserable she was and asking when I was going to call on her ...

Well, the ending is not bad, **but I had told her, like all of the great girls I had met, that I was a San Francisco boy and I would return there and decide my life from that viewpoint.**

When I was in San Antonio, a girlfriend wanted me to have a photograph taken. She convinced me to go to a professional photographer. This is the picture I got. At first I thought I was lop-sided, then I was convinced by the photographer that this was the way the Hollywood stars took their picture. First I came to like it, then I started to think I was good-looking, then I sent the picture home. I forgot all about this picture until I was almost finished with the book and the picture showed up. Somebody told me I looked like Gene Kelly, then I really took off. Oh well, wish me luck in Hollywood.

Chapter 32

My Most Embarrassing Moment

Do you remember in some of my early chapters I talked about growing up and about having an inferiority complex? Well, as I grew up, I did not get embarrassed as much, or even think about it.

Well, there was one time I went out with my new pal, Vince, who was with me a short time in Texas. Master Sergeant Vince was going with a governor's daughter and he fixed me up a date with one of her girlfriends to go swimming in a most beautiful place in Texas ... **the swimming area was huge and the long pool was built like many things in Texas — BIG!**

My buddy Vince fixed everything up. Now, I was about 22 or 23, and you would think age would not make a difference. Well, think again! Old Benny Sent Me was a basket case. The other guys would have given an arm and leg to be set up for this kind of a date ... the girls had the food ... there was no cost ... and now, looking back, I would give an arm and leg to be single and have the same opportunity (only kidding!) ... oh well, live and learn!

Now, the girl was a school teacher ... she was nice-looking, clean as a whistle, educated, built nicely ... other GI's would jump at the chance, and GI's just coming home would hop, skip, and jump at the chance for this kind of date. Me, I was thinking some people would think, gee, I was out with my mother ... the girl must have been 25 or 27, and here, I was only 22 ... I must be desperate!!!

The poor girl would swim near me, and I would immediately start swimming to the other end of the pool ... how mean could I get ... this was not only stupid, it was double stupid; but when you are young and stupid it is triple stupid. It was one of those hot summer days in Texas, so staying in the water was a nice place to be. I don't think the others thought or knew what I was doing and how I felt.

Now, you see, most people would not tell about this event in their life, but I wanted you to know that all through the War, I was not desperate; I was not hungry ... I was just the way I was in high school or college. I was waiting for my time to come. I wanted to do it my way.

After the swimming, we did things that did not involve other people seeing or being with me, and I relaxed and was more my natural self. I ended up with a great day. My pal Vince was in his glory with the daughter of a governor ... he could tell his parents or his friends that he spent his day with such notables. Me ... I felt like a rat. Hey, I was a rat and, let's face it, **that's exactly why Mickey Mouse left home; he found out his father was a rat!**

Now, the place we went to that day had beautiful gardens ... Today, I'm sure you would have to pay to go through them. As for old Vince, I never did follow up on him after the War. I have researched this after-the-war business and found out, from almost everyone I asked, that they never contacted or wrote to or visited any of their buddies from the War. This leads me to think that after the War all of us were emotionally spent ... **we did not want to think about the War, we did not want to read about the War, and we did not want to talk about the War.**

About that day in Texas ... as Mae West used to say, "You done me wrong." I really did that lovely day in Texas wrong and I admit it. If ever I get to Texas ... say, for example, I make a small fortune on this book, like enough to pay for a trip back there to research all the places I have been ... maybe I would go back, although I'd have to admit, I probably wouldn't. I used to know a guy in the Army that always told me, **"Never chew the same tobacco twice."** He was right the first time, because I never chew tobacco, and he would be right the second time, because I never chewed tobacco in the first place, and in other words ... another Abbott & Costello routine ... see you in another chapter when I will make more sense.

There is nothing more important in the Service than mail call. This picture was taken in the Adjutant General's section of Fort Sam Houston, in San Antonio, Texas, where we would go after a cup of coffee, to get our mail.

Mail call was more important than "Chow." We used to write to each other, many times, just so we wouldn't get a "no mail" when our name was called. Buddies, children, parents, sweethearts, everyone was asked to send letters.

When I arrived at Fort Sam Houston, we would go for the mail, collect it, then run across the street to a drug store, have a cup of coffee, and figure out the entire war while we read our mail.

In the picture, I am on the right-hand side. The only thing wrong with being home (meaning the States) was that there were hardly any promotions. All these were saved for the returning veterans.

I think we understood that part. There were mixed emotions in out headquarters. We might have been happy not to be in combat, but who were we to choose? Many of our staff constantly went to the top of headquarters to secure overseas duty, but the people running the war were scared stiff to lose our type of personnel. We were trained to send troops overseas, trained to get them back, trained for whatever we did. It is too bad; they finally got around to getting women and almost at the end of the war, they made a class of office people that could do office work but were unable to do military combat duty. That would have eased the guilt feelings that prevailed.

Chapter 33

Ike Could Have Been a Contender — Patton Pays Ben a Visit

Some chapters ago I explained to you about my experience at the Presidio of San Francisco. There I was taught all the tricks of being an excellent records clerk, because when you are working for generals and they want some information, you had better find it, but quick.

Well, I did not realize what I was learning at that time was what the finest librarian has to know: just where everything is, when you or the other person wants it. First of all, none of the clerks I knew ever knew the Dewey Decimal System. That is the system that classifies just about every item; no matter what, where, or why, you can still find it. It was fun for me ... but then again, I did not come across many college graduates doing records.

Now I want you to remember when I told you about the grocery store ... it was my good fortune to be born enjoying everything I do or did. I enjoyed figuring out what was what. To me, doing true recording of records was an art, and no matter how much work it was, I always said, I did it the hard way or I did it my way.

You know, during the War, my favorite general was Eisenhower. **Everyone liked Ike. I liked Ike.** I felt Eisenhower was too good and never received all the credit due him. All the generals from England and the other Allied generals were praised, while Eisenhower just kept negotiating ... not criticizing like the others. Ike kept America a partner, and joined or agreed in almost everything Churchill and England proposed.

The bombing at Pearl Harbor ended all resistance, and America was suddenly deep into the war effort. America put on one of the most exhilarating production efforts ever seen in world history. The bulletins were coming out of the War Department in droves ... cut electricity, cut auto production, cut, cut, cut. It was electrifying to read, see, or do, but the world was not going to lose to the Nazis or Japanese, no matter what. Remember I told you, I had just gotten out of University of California, so I was more into the excitement of watching history being made, rather than deep into the fighting. I always said, we all contribute in our own way. I was involved in the War up to my elbows; but it was not physical, it was mental.

Well, General Eisenhower, with his ability to compromise, cooperate, and manage the war effort, was a joy to me. Ike was a leader, and he proved it both in war and peace. Yep, I liked Ike! Now, when General Eisenhower, with his ability to lead, was given a chance, he produced his armies. Almost no one had ever managed General Patton, but Ike chose him in the big drive in Europe. General Patton was the greatest fighting general. He knew no fear and actually loved the fighting rather than the negotiations and strategy business ... he loved the battle.

The Seventh Army, under General Patton, produced a drive that no one, including Ike and the War Department, dreamed could happen. He moved like lightning and had to be detained so as to not embarrass the other armies in the same area.

In one of his drives, General Patton visited the Army hospital; in his attempt to shock an enlisted man into not being afraid, he slapped him, thinking the shock would get him back to normal ... It backfired, and in a matter of minutes it was news. The newspapers picked this up and spread it all over the world. The War Department had so many letters and telephone calls, plus the pressure of the press was too great, so Eisenhower was told to settle this difficult matter.

The easiest way to handle General Patton was to send him back to America and let things cool off ... The only Army headquarters in America was now the 4th Army Headquarters in San Antonio, Texas. Right smack where I was stationed! He arrived with great press coverage and excitement, and he immediately advised that all enlisted men and officers would be called for a special meeting in the Quadrangle at Fort Sam Houston, to listen to what General Patton had to say.

We issued these orders right in my department. So General Patton gave his speech and the entire group of officers and enlisted men listened to the great General talk. It was exciting ... however, General Patton was subdued and had to state that he could not have any more incidents and would appreciate it if anyone having a problem, no matter how trivial, would contact his office, so that there would be no further problem for General George Patton.

A day or two later, General Patton visited the Records Division, where I worked. We knew he was on his way, as information like that travels faster than lightning. First thing I knew, General Patton came right to the counter where I was and asked for copies of yesterday's talk. **I handed it to him in 5 seconds flat ... I was so excited, it was almost 5 seconds**

flat on my back! ...But **General Patton called me by name; he said, "Thank you, Soldier** — you did a good job." I was sky high with adrenaline running through me. I will never forget that day. It was my most exciting moment ... it was a moment of history in my life.

General Patton Comes to Fourth Army Headquarters

This picture was taken on the day we were to listen to General George Patton for the first time. It was shortly after the story broke in all of the world papers that General Patton had slapped a soldier overseas in a hospital. It was his opinion that his act would produce beneficial effects. Unfortunately, the world was stunned and it produced opposite results. General Eisenhower was forced to calm the public. General Patton was sent home for rest and a change of scenery. He was assigned to the Fourth Army in San Antonio, Texas.

It was in this speech that General Patton pleaded with all of us in the Fourth Army to not write letters home or talk to news correspondents without talking to him personally. We were on notice to see him with any complaints we might have or problems that could be settled. In a way this led to my first leave home to San Francisco. The story is in one of the chapters of "My Silent Partner." See if you can locate me in the picture!

Chapter 34

Some Sunday Morning

This is going to be the saddest chapter in the book ... Believe it or not, I can't recall one Sunday morning in the Army which I actually devoted to the Lord. It got to be just one Sunday after another. Even with me not being in a combat unit or close to death, my mind never paid attention to the day. I cannot, in all honesty, remember one Sunday that I actually devoted to prayer. What a shame! What happened to my religious upbringing? I went to a Catholic grammar school, my mother and grandmother were great with the religious feelings, and here for the life of me, I can't remember what I did on Sundays.

You know, I believe that when you are in your early twenties, you feel brave and do not even think of dying or death. Let's go over things ... from the time I went to College of Pacific, I never went to church on Sunday. Now I guess maybe I thought I did not need the Lord.

Then take University of California ... nothing. I don't even remember any conversations or discussions about the Lord. At that time, there were a lot of nutty type of people — people who challenged the world at that stage of life. I was too busy for that, but I wonder if any other people did what I did (or didn't do) ... to think I didn't have one religious thought or feeling! You know, I can't recall even one thing that brought me to my senses ... was I challenging the world?

I probably won't print this chapter because the Lord is the only thing I think about that really counts, and I am ashamed to tell you about all of this. I only hope there were others like me, so I won't feel like it is the end of the world. You know that this book is dedicated to the Good Lord ... maybe my Silent Partner will forgive me this one time.

The only explanation I have to offer is that the War consumed everyone ... there were very few exceptions. My heart goes out to those that had children that were injured or killed. I am sure that they prayed a lot. I am going to end this poor substitute of a chapter with the feeling that I have the rest of my life to pray and help others, and that is exactly what I intend to do, so help me God. So ... Help me, God.

May 29, 1995. Today is Sunday and I am looking at all of the movies on Memorial Day, and it hit me like a ton of bricks ... and guess what? I have watched every USO segment: all of the movie stars selling bonds; every famous person in the entire world, selling bonds, raising money, and trying to help America during World War II. They didn't leave anyone out either ... Here was Dorothy Lamour, Bob Hope, Bing Crosby, Danny Kaye, Jimmy Durante, Abbott & Costello, Jimmy Cagney, Judy Garland. **You name him or her, and you saw what they were doing for America ... and I'll bet not one of them went to church that Sunday!** It was a gigantic showing of the War and I was continually in tears ... 50 years ago, and I still cry about it.

There was a movie segment of the famous swimmer, Esther Williams ... the one that made all those famous swim pictures. She had bet she would swim with any GI and, if she lost, she would give him a big kiss. Well, a GI with only one leg and one arm raises his hand, and everyone there is crying, and she lets him beat her ... talk about tears!

Now, I was more determined to do this chapter than before ... and I'll tell you why. I realized the world did not like what it was going through. People did not like all the sadness of the war. They realized that war was terrible, inhuman, and destructive ... but they thought we had to do everything we could, so that maybe we would have a future. Even the religious establishments closed their eyes and silently prayed. Nobody wanted to mention religion because of the great conflict between killing and religion. All our lives were at stake. Everyone wanted the War to end, and end so we would have the ability to pray that we would have guys like me and My Silent Partner around to help the world.

You know, I am crying as I write this, because I realize that I almost left out the chapter that is the most important. Too bad ... Yes, too bad if I don't make you laugh in this chapter. And almost too bad I even had those thoughts.

Today is Memorial Day and it is May 29, 1995, about 50 years after WWII, the big one. Hey, no matter how little a part my Silent Partner and I played fifty years ago, I think He saved a person that will always want to do good, no matter what ... so be it said in His name.

Chapter 35

Whatta You Gonna Do
When the War is Over?

You know, as the War was getting close to being over, lot of guys were starting to think, "What do I do when I get back home?" I used to ask the guys all the time, "Charlie, what are you gonna do when you get home?" "Oh," he'd say, "I'm gonna eat Polish sausage and sauerkraut; then I'll figure out what I want to do." Next case: "Hey, Joe ... You live in Chicago; what are you going to do when you get home?" "Oh," he'd say, "I'm gonna eat ravioli and lasagne till I drop." Gee, I was really asking, "What are we gonna do for a living?"

Me, I used to lie in the bunk, wide awake ... I never slept much because I never did much — I mean physically. So I would wake up with all these different ideas, thoughts, whatever came into my mind. I liked thinking I was going to be a comedian, and all sorts of jokes would snap into my brain. I had just started telling everyone I went four days straight without any sleep ... nobody would believe me and they would all say the same thing: "Maybe you are worried about going home"; "Maybe you are nervous about the War," etc., etc., Then I would give them the rest of the joke: **"I haven't slept in four days, but thank goodness I sleep at night; otherwise, I would be a physical wreck!"**

Then I would tell jokes about the war like: **"I got this bump in the War"** ... and the other guys would say, **"What war? What bump? You never got this in any war!" And I would say, "I mean the boud-war."**

Then I figured I could go on the talent shows and I could make up a monologue like: **"A guy goes into a grocery store and says, 'I want a can of kiddley beans,'** and the grocer says, **'You mean kidney beans?'** and the guy says, **'That's what I said, diddle I?'"** I could follow this with: **"An Italian guy goes into a store and yells, 'Stick 'em down!'** and the owner says, **'You mean stick 'em up, don't you?'** ... and the Italian guy says, **'No wonder I don't make-a much money!'"** ... Oh well, these were thoughts; I figured the kind of stuff I was hearing on the radio was no better than my stuff ... then I would really wake up and tell myself it was only a dream.

Then, during my spare time, I would ask myself, "Could I really be a comedian?" I couldn't memorize a monologue; I couldn't even spell monologue, let along memorize one! I never could memorize even phone numbers; somehow, that is not what I am good at.

Come to think of it, I was not good at many things ... let's face it, I was a lousy soldier; I was a lousy sports guy — I couldn't play tennis, baseball, handball, swim; you name it and I wasn't good at it. I was lousy at mathematics; I wasn't too good a dancer; I was terrible at directions and a million other things. Now, that was the bad side. Now, look at the good side: I was a good talker; I was a good cook; I was honest; and I loved religion and the Bible. Gee, I guess that's quite a bit for me. Anyway, I had told myself I would do only what I was good at and try to be the best at what I did ... Oh yes, I was pretty good at writing; you had better read this book and like it or I am sunk! And another thing: on big things I was lucky, such as family life; getting along with people ... these things I was good at and, as I have told you in almost every chapter, I was happy or I made myself happy; **I am not one of those guys that has to have the whole salami — just a piece of the pie is good enough for me!** With these points out of the way, let us proceed ...

Now, what was I going to do when I got out of the Army? I was so used to the Army after 40 months of service. I thought I would lose all my friends or girlfriends I had while in the Army. I never fell in love; I always said I wanted to marry a girl from San Francisco and raise my family in San Francisco and, so far, everything has been right ... I had the big scare with the four wires in my brain, but my pal and Silent Partner took care of that matter, and here I am writing to you all, as they say in Texas.

Hey, let's get back to What Am I Going to Do When the War is Over? I had plans that I will not reveal in this book, only in my next book, which will be entitled "I Went Broke in the Boom." Stay alive so you can buy it, and as usual, **The Price is Right.**

Now, here it was near the end of the War and I had not been home in almost two years. As a sergeant now, I was surrounded by master sergeants that had been returned from combat duty and were sitting all around me, waiting to get discharged. We were almost at the close of the War, when I spotted a bulletin going through, stating that if you had not had a furlough for a long time and felt you needed one, you could ask for three weeks; you could ask for one, and if conditions called for it, you could get one.

Gee, I thought I should try for a three-week furlough. So I went to Harry, the one that could make the decision, and he told me I was crazy. Now, he didn't know Benny; like my mother used to say, I was going to be a lawyer ... I pleaded my case that I had had no vacation in two years, I didn't know what my family looked like anymore, and that this was the appropriate time. This Sergeant Harry wanted to give me ten days, which was more than a week ... (that is what Harry said). I showed him the bulletin and Harry said if he gave me a three-week furlough, every guy in the Army would ask for the same thing. I told Harry, "Not every guy in the Army will know about this and I am sure you can do it." **He procrastinated longer than I took to figure out how to spell "procrastinated."** He said he would give me two weeks ... then the zinger came. Remember when I said that General Patton, who was now the head at Headquarters Fourth Army, had stated that if anyone was unhappy, he could ask to speak to General Patton? Well, I pulled out that article to show Master Sergeant Harry and said I was going to ask to speak to General Patton. Now, you and I know that I would NOT do that in a million years, but Sergeant Harry did not know that ... he told me he would ask the Captain what he should do, and the next day, I was the first guy in San Antonio that had a three-week pass!

Now, the ending of this story is not what you think. I got home and found out I missed out on my grandfather's funeral, as the family said they did not want me to come home for something like that. So Tata was gone. I did not know who to call to take out or date ... I was a total stranger in my home town.

All my friends were in the Service. Nine-tenths of all the places you could have gone to before the War were out of business or not open. I was lost! What a miserable three weeks I had at home! I worked in the store and saw all my close relatives, but other than that, I just killed time. It was a big surprise to me and I asked myself this question: WHAT AM I GOING TO DO WHEN THE WAR IS OVER?!!

This picture was taken on the day I was promoted to sergeant. It took over three years to get a promotion. There were so many returnees, the Army would put five master sergeants in our office. I guess we were considered lucky to be in the States, rather than in combat. That was not true, but we had no choice in the matter. By the time I explained to five master sergeants what the job was, the War was over and we were on our way home!!!

Chapter 36

Born on the Fourth of July

This year, 1995, our father, who art in heaven, would have been 100 years old ... Sister Roberta, or Bert, asked me if we would like to have a get-together in his honor. How I left this out of the book on Papa, I'll never know, because it was such a big event every year of his life, and I never said a word until Roberta mentioned his famous birthday ... this year on July 4th he would have been 100 years of age.

Every year, the relatives would all call up Mary and ask if Robert was going to have the fireworks, and every year my mother would tell them to come on over and we would have some dinner and stuff right after he finished with his display.

Papa always would say, "I bought a lot of firecrackers and new fireworks, and we can play cards and the kids can sing on the piano with the rolls." This was fun for all of us, and all those old-time songs that are still popular today were there for us to sing. My mother, Mary, just loved to cook, and all the relatives and friends loved to pitch in to make the Fourth of July a special day for our father. All the women would look out the window and my father would kneel down and light the fuse for the special fireworks ... every year they got more complicated and interesting to watch. Remember, this was out in the street ... Papa would light the fuse and run like sixty and get all the little ones out of the way. This went on for about an hour, until Papa would run out of ammunition, and this is not a joke, but the real thing.

My mother would have cooked all kinds of pasta; pizza; chow-chow, which would be considered like the Mexican salsa of today; braciole (thin slices of round steak with a bread stuffing) ... Oh, we had just about anything you wanted to eat. **Food was never the problem; eating too much was** ... So our entire life, we enjoyed the Fourth of July thanks to Papa's birthday.

Papa always had to tell us the story of when he went to get his citizenship papers. The judge was interviewing him, and in the old days, they wanted the new citizen to feel what a wonderful thing it was to become an American citizen ... and it really was a wonderful thing. This judge saw on his papers that Papa was born on the Fourth of July, so he asked my father if he knew what the Fourth of July stood for, and my father replied, "That's my birthday." Papa always told this little event so great; I couldn't begin to show you his expression, plus how proud he was to be an American.

You know, Papa never talked about Italy. Others always tried to build up Italy and make you think it was better than America ... not my dad. He was American 1000 percent, and he kept up with politics and all the latest news.

Remember when I said in this book that there was something my father had that was special, although I, personally, always stuck up for my mother and never chose my father's side? Now I realize how he molded the family ... he never turned down education or knowledge over money; money to my dad was bad news, bad medicine, bad luck. I can honestly say I inherited that from Papa ... too bad we don't get a second chance in life.

One year, Papa had his Fourth of July party at my grandmother's house. Now that building was three floors, and Nana's floor was on top. From the third floor you could go on the roof, so we could watch the fireworks from three floors up. That year Papa had obtained some fancy fireworks for this birthday ... I believe it might have been the last year of the war. Anyway, evidently one of the fireworks was not igniting or something. The family and other relatives were watching from the windows and suddenly saw Papa fainting, so they ran downstairs three flights and pulled him away from the fireworks. They forgot about fireworks and revived Papa, who had apparently passed out from inhalation of fumes.

As the War was ending, I guess people were a little tired of fireworks and had had enough for a long time to come. Later, big fireworks were shown in the Marina district, and we would go up on the roof to see them in the sky, just like you would at Disneyland today. Every year Papa's famous birthday was a big event. So my sister Roberta had this idea of celebrating this July 4th as the 100th year of Papa's life ... You'll just have to read about it in our next book!

This picture shows my mother and father on their 50th anniversary. If you look closely, my father has his masonic pin on his lapel. This caused a lot of arguments in our family because somehow, without real knowledge, my mother always thought that it was not right for my dad to be a Shriner. Yet my father said to me he felt that there was more religion in his lodge than he saw in all of the Catholic churches he went to for all the Italian weddings, christenings and funerals.

Chapter 37

The Bridges of San Fran

You don't know this, but I nearly finished this entire book when I suddenly remembered that the Bridges of San Francisco were left out ... there was NO way that I could complete this book without the "Bridges of San Fran", and I will tell you why. One bridge was completed in 1937, and that was the year I graduated from Galileo High School. All you heard from all over the world were the magnificent Bridges of San Fran. **People were coming from all over to see the fascinating two bridges that were captivating the engineering world and had made San Francisco famous.**

On one side we had the Golden Gate Bridge and on the other side, we had the San Francisco Bay Bridge ... It was awesome. The Bay Bridge had a long entrance approach, so you could enjoy the approach and view on the bridge. We walked with all the other kids on the Bay Bridge, as both bridges were being completed, almost at the same time. And you know, Galileo High School was only blocks away from the Golden Gate Bridge!

The Golden Gate Bridge was so close to our store and home, you could see both bridges going up, right from the roof of our home ... what a sight to see! They were about two miles away, well within walking distance. It was like watching an erector set ... each day the view was different. Every day the papers had new articles ... someone hurt, complications in the building ... it was a way to keep you interested. Sort of like the soap operas of today!

Soon the Bay Bridge was ready. Then, in 1937, came the Golden Gate ... all kinds of parades, movies, speakers all ready to explain to the entire world the building of the bridges. It was a beauty to behold.

When I went to University of California at Berkeley, I would take the train right through the San Francisco Bay Bridge. Most students would be studying for their classes that they had for that day ... not me; I was oblivious to U.C. Berkeley. I guess it did not have a high priority with me. Don't ask me why, because I was practically flunking out at the time. I would be in awe, every single trip to U.C. campus across the bridge.

Many times I sat with an Italian fellow named Vic on the train and we would talk sports, instead of school. Little did I know he and his brother would become partners as the first owners of the San

Francisco 49ers ... what a small world! Victor and Tony Morabito were co-owners of the present World Champions of Pro-Football.

I told you before that I did not enjoy University of California ... but it wasn't the school ... it was the war which was coming, and was here before I graduated. My brother Rich had a low number in the draft and he was drafted right away. When he left, the store became sort of my responsibility. I used to work after the three days a week I went to Cal ... I used to work all day Tuesday, Thursday, Saturday, and Sundays. I was so used to this life, I did not realize there were other things in life. My grades in school deteriorated; my interest waned.

Soon war was all around us. Rationing started in the foods right away ... sugar, coffee, meats, and one thing after another ... all the shortages brought on problems. I graduated, just barely ... and even though these things were happening, we still had the San Francisco World Fair. Treasure Island was created, and was the forerunner of Disneyland. They built this island, right near the bridges and you could get to Treasure Island from both of the bridges and also the ferry boats ... what a fun area for a dismal world ... but we could not think of bad things, only that we had this Treasure Island just miles away. Entertainers came daily. Celebrities wanted to see the beauties of the World's Fair and all kinds of dance bands, shows, and the great Cavalcade of Stars.

We all used to go on the ferries, where you could dance and enjoy the ferry boat ride. It was a place to go to enjoy yourself in spite of the war-torn world around us. Just before going back home, we used to go to the Maxwell House Coffee shop for great donuts and hot coffee ... made right before your eyes. Meanwhile, if you walked on Market Street, the biggest street in San Francisco, you could see the sailors coming in for shore leave, a grim reminder of the oncoming winds of war ...

San Francisco was a seaport city, and many sailors and Marine officers would be browsing around the famous Market Street, which led to the Ferry Building. As many sailors, away from home, were lost and only followed everyone else on Market Street, there were a lot of bars and girls looking for excitement. One thing I will recall ... despite the crowds, despite the excitement and despite the War, no scandals arose from Market Street ... people were serious and the world was beginning to get serious.

The Bridges of San Fran were new to us and to the world ... Starting in 1937 people came from all over the world to see the streets of San Francisco. Think of what happened after the War ... the bridges opened up a new world, and there was an exodus to the neighboring areas for many reasons — San Francisco's weather, the cost of living, and the lack of space. In nearby communities, people could find warmer weather and lower prices, start a new life, and still work in the city.

The Bridges of San Fran opened up the beauty of San Francisco to the entire world. People from near and far still come to enjoy the cool weather and pretty sights. The bridges of San Francisco are part of the magic of the Bay Area ... no story would be complete without explaining one of the greatest engineering feats of the 20th Century.

Well, I was back in this beautiful city and ready to start my life anew!

Chapter 38

The Birthday Bomb: August 9th

The atomic bomb was thrown on Nagasaki on my birthday, August 9th. A few days later Japan surrendered and the rest was history. The War was over!

I was stationed at Fort Sam Houston in San Antonio at the time. I had just returned from my three-week furlough that I told you about in a previous chapter. I had felt so funny during that vacation, as no one was around ... all my buddies were in the Service. My grandfather had already passed away. I had just worked around the store, as my prior life had always centered on the store.

V-J Day, the end of the War against Japan, was different than V-E Day. **On V-E Day**, when the War against Europe ended, **we were halfway home, but on V-J Day, it was the end of the end. On V-E Day we were looking to celebrate. On V-J Day we were looking to or thinking of the future.**

For the life of me, I can't remember what I did on V-J Day, but when the biggie came, I was ready for it. Remember I told you I had that guilty feeling during the latter part of the War, because everyone else was into it and I was still home. I had absolutely NOTHING to do with my still being in the U.S.A.; it was just one of those flukes. It seemed that every time it looked like I was going to be called for overseas duty, my name was taken off the list. I recall one time where my name was on a departing list and, in a few hours, some general at Fort Sam Houston had it taken off because he needed personnel to do the paper work there. Oh well, **in life sometimes even a little guy on the team wins the game for our side!**

So when V-J Day took place, I was back at Fort Sam Houston, surrounded by master sergeants. They were all coming home, with nothing to do but wait for the War to end. I was now a sergeant, but the only one in the section that really knew what keeping records and files was all about ... it was like working in a library, and I was custodian of any record anyone needed or wanted to see. Maybe that is why I can't recall exactly what I did on V-J Day — I was knee-deep in records!

Now, the big talk was, "What do I do now that the War is over?" I would say 99 percent did not know, except that they wanted to go home. I needed to stay in San Antonio and await my legal discharge. My brother Rich got home first, as all the overseas soldiers were given first priority and were being sent home by the hundreds of thousands. I was one of the last to leave, as I had to help the discharged people get their orders for home.

Rich had already taken his insurance broker's license exam, but I still had to take my test when I got home. I studied for the exam, went to City Hall, and got my license. I remember how wonderful people were and how they would show their gratitude in certain ways. I was close on the exam, but I was a couple of multiple-choice questions off. The testing officer, knowing I was a serviceman, asked if maybe I had misread or misunderstood these couple of questions and gave me a chance to change my answers. Naturally, I said, "Oh yeah, that's what I meant," and he passed me. In those days, it was no big deal ... today, the Insurance Department in California is so rough, the brokers are dying on the vines. So I was a real live insurance broker!

I remember we had about 18 policies in force, and I can tell you ahead of time that in our first year of business we had two months, our second and fourth months, where we grossed $100.00 in total commissions ... Wow! Imagine how little that was, but we knew we were on our way. Our parents had given us $5,000.00 to start the business, as we had to find a company to represent; we had to find an office; we had to get going.

Inflation was starting up, with the new action of the returnees. The street car next to our house increased the fare to 10 cents, from 5 cents, and we walked for about a week in protest.

We found an insurance company that would give us an office, office supplies, and a phone if we did our business with them. So we signed up with the Traveler's Insurance Company. We were on our way!

One of the first things I did was go to a business school that taught you how to be a good public speaker. I remember I had to start each sentence, practically, with a question, or a startling statement, or another of seven choices they gave us. I got a good grade, but this was a commercial business and they saw to it that we all were given a good grade in something along the line, so we would not get discouraged or quit the course. It was FREE for service men, and that is why I brought this up ... the entire country was trying to help us get started. We also got a subsidy for a year or two of $100.00 or $200.00 per month if we were making less than what they considered a normal amount. **All along the line, the country was being fair to the returning servicemen.**

Chapter 39

See Us Freeze

About the time I returned from World War II, the bakery across the street from our store and home was sold, and an ice cream store, "See Us Freeze," moved in ... it was a new idea. You could watch the different flavors being made from outside or inside the store. The kids would stay for hours and stare from outside the window. Right after the War, we welcomed anything different. People wanted change, and they were getting it with "See Us Freeze."

We were about fifty years behind. People sensed change all around us. The idea was so great, as young kids and their parents loved to watch the ice cream being made right before their eyes. The ice cream maker sort of looked like a washing machine on "spin" drive. I can't believe how much we were behind in the world ... Don't ask me why, but we realized the world wasn't moving slow any more. It was a new world. So when this store opened up, it was a novelty ... you could See Us Freeze, freezing the ice cream.

Somehow this new guy would come into our grocery store and talk to me. I was always foolin' around with the fruit and produce section, which was 90% of our business. He kept asking me to remind him when the bananas got real ripe, or the raspberries or strawberries were getting to the stage where we might want to get rid of them. You see, in those days we did not have refrigeration, and no air conditioning. **When our produce and fruit ripened it was "goodbye," "adios," "see you later alligator!"** We had to throw the stuff away. But my new friend Earle, the young owner of See Us Freeze, would blend the fruit at its most flavorful stage, into the electric machine that you could see from outside the store.

It was fun to see the different flavors being produced like magic, as we waited to see what the next concoction would be. Earle had a phobia about leaving his job at City Hall, and risking his job (probably about $200.00 per month at that time), for this ice cream store. Imagine him asking me for advice! I was about ten years younger, and he would talk about this every time we got together. I kept telling Earle that he was crazy to worry, and with his talent in making all these new ice cream concoctions he was really a genius. Way ahead of his time. In those days there were no companies like International Fruit and Flavors ... it was all the "real McCoy." I don't even know if there was a "Federal Drug Administration" at that time.

Well, Earle started putting signs like they do in vaudeville, where they slide in the sign to show the next act. You could see the name of the ice cream he was making, and they all had great names ... like "Banana Nut Supreme," or "Orange Tango," "Thin Mint," "Lemon Drop," or "Lemon Flake Sherbet." Now, these are my names, but they were something like that.

Earle was old-fashioned, and his father and mother, or younger brother, or whatever relative, was always working with him in the See Us Freeze store. Guess what ... the prices, when he started, were a nickel or a dime, at the most. And for a dime, they put it in a carton and maybe you got syrup on top, or more than one scoop. For the public, it was fun to stick around at Union and Hyde Streets. It became a tourist treat, as Cable Cars were run by two men, and they would stop and run into the store, get a cone, and then get back in the car and jingle their bells. It was a treat.

Now this took place only fifty feet from our home and store. From the "Aeroplane Room," you could hear the Cable Car conductors playing their bells, or the sound of their brakes. It became a showboat thing ... a San Francisco tourist attraction.

Back to See Us Freeze ... his main purchase from our store was always bananas. It was one of his best sellers. And now we revert back to our mother. She was afraid of anything that moved. A mouse, a dog, a cat. If it moved, she was afraid of it. Whenever we left the store or went off to school, mama always said, "Watch out for the dog." We all became paranoiac about stuff like that. So some news comes out that sometimes, even after bananas are put through fumigation, some of the tarantulas hidden deep in the banana bunches escape. So every time that Earle would ask for bananas, or wanted bananas, I was afraid I'd wind up with a tarantula killing me! I always used to say to Earle, "You cut off the bananas you like, and I or my father will tell you how much you owe us!" I will always remember Earle, and "See Us Freeze." He was a man ahead of his time ... the inventor of "watch-us-make-it" fresh fruit ice cream. Sometimes I wonder, should he have left his city job, or gone back to protect his "leave of absence"?!

Chapter 40

The End of the Beginning

I thought I would save the last chapter for an analysis on Ben, alias Benjie, alias Benny Sent Me, and/or just plain Benny ... I never could make up my mind on any one of these, but as the old saying was, **"I don't care what name you call me, but don't call me too late for dinner!"** I thought, after thinking of all that I have written, you would like some self-analysis on my strengths and weaknesses. I will start on all of my weaknesses, as that will leave me able to pick up good thoughts for my final conclusions.

My original fears or weaknesses from the very beginning were that I thought I had an inferiority complex. I thought I was not quite sharply coordinated; I only had my brother Richie to judge by, and at an early age, 17 months difference is great. The difference between the two of us would appear in things like running and agility .... So that was a weak spot.

Then we get into the brain ... I was not good in any mathematical calculations or arithmetic ... definitely not very good marks could I chalk up there.

Then we have my complexion; I thought dark-complected people did not rate as highly with the female sex, and I was dark-complected ... A minus there.

I was not sharp in baseball; playing the piano; war or combat drills like shooting, target practice, things of a physical nature ... Another minus there. Then fear of not being liked by the female sex did not exactly help.

I never liked to drive; I didn't even drive until I was 19 years old, and I have no sense of direction. Even today, I get lost in San Francisco, and it is only 7 miles in any direction ... that is a big minus. I guess that is about it, as far as my minus production goes.

Now, what do I do that makes me proud or happy, or gives me a feeling of success, or justifies my even writing this stupid self-analysis? Why do I even want to reveal all my plus and minus qualities? Just to prove to you that there is a lot more in store for you. I plan a trilogy and have at least two more books that I know you will enjoy. One, I will tell you ahead of time, will be great fun and laughter and tears. It will be a book called "I Went Broke in the Boom" and you will wonder a million times in that book why I didn't do what a normal person would have done. It will really make you wonder about my plus-and-minus column, as the stock market is all about plus and minus ... so get ready for that book. I predict it will be a great book in the financial and fun fields. Then, the final book will be glad and sad, and we will face that when the time comes ...

Now we talk about my good points ... right off the bat, the fact that I can cry over everything and anything and still bounce back ... yes, I feel that is a big plus. My ability to bounce back ... I always think like Scarlett O'Hara in "Gone with the Wind." "Tomorrow ... things will be better tomorrow." I can't reveal some big sorrows I have had, but you will hear them ... rest assured of that.

So many people hold grudges; I know a lot of Italians that pride themselves on how many people they don't talk to, like that is an asset. Anyway, I love everyone. Too bad I can't say everyone deserves to be loved, but I forget about it because there are so many good things and people in the world ... no big deal.

Now for my biggest asset. That is my love for God. The Lord has already spared me for this book. It was only months ago ... I was about to enter a "new world," until I was spared and given another chance to do what I like best, and that is to write. The Lord and I will show you how great it is to love Him every second, minute, hour, day of your life, and the rest is all secondary. I want to always rest my decision with the Good Lord, and remember ... He is My Silent Partner, so you had better not cross me or Him.

I can talk about almost everything and if I can't, maybe I can fake it ... so long as it doesn't hurt anyone. In this book, there will be times when you say to yourself, "What is this guy talking about? It never happened that way," or "He is just making the book sound good." Like my love for Galileo High School ... just last week I got a call from a school buddy and he said he heard that I was writing this book and he wants to see a couple chapters so he can help me with some of his memories ... It never ceases.

I have enough material to last a lifetime, and I will never run out (of material). When I finish telling the truth, then I will write fiction. My daughter, Marilyn, who is working so hard to make this first book a success, tells me, "Gosh, Dad, how can you remember all these things and places and events?" And do you know what I told my daughter? "If I can interest you or the public with real things and make them interesting, imagine what I can do if I have the ability to make it come out the way all would like it to come out?"

Now that I realize that being a little dark-complected was no liability, that is over with and done. My talking ability stood me in good grace all through my life, and I became a good storyteller and good joke teller, and all my liabilities became assets. The only thing I can tell you is: **God so made the world that you always need Him.** Remember that, if you don't remember anything else in this book. It has helped me to know that **win, lose, or draw, I would rather win ... but if I can't win, I hope to come in second. If I can't come in second, the heck with it ... I still have the Lord, and He is always in First Place.**

I want to make one last comment to all of you. The stories or things I have commented on were, as best as I could state, the truth. I am not a very reliable person when it comes to places, dates, and things, but the events in this book happened and I did not make anything up, except a few corny jokes that are in this book. I don't know if I was exact or nearly correct on the details, but **if you write as many words as I did in this book, I would like to see *your* report card.**

So this is the beginning of the end, or the the ending of the beginning ... or is it the beginning of the beguine? Should I ask Artie Shaw how to spell the beginning of the beguine? Or maybe this is the beginning of more than ONE ending!

Chapter 41

The Last Hurrah

Believe me, this last chapter has taken me almost as long to write as the entire book. Don't ask me why, because I have written this chapter thirty-nine different ways, and it still does not satisfy me. This is the last hurrah!

First of all, the book started about our little grocery store, went into our family life, detoured a few chapters ... then into Galileo High School. That's when I started to really enjoy writing the book. Each night or so, I remembered more of my past. Now that I'm almost finished, my mind blanks out. Maybe it is because I don't want the book to end. Or maybe I wore my thinking cap out. Or it is that I have no experience in ending a story ... You know, that just might be it!

It is starting to dawn on me about my personality ... I was never the one to end the conversation. I always wanted the story, or the conversation to NEVER end. It was the ideal part of my life, when I was talking, writing, or enjoying being with people. Yes, that was it. It came to me in a flash!

So that was it ... the "Last Hurrah." The finish. The end. Just like in the movies. The doctor figures out the reason for the whole story. I remember Ingrid Bergman in a movie with Charles Boyer called "Gaslight," and how the mind works ... and in Stanley Kramer's "Home of the Brave," where the guy goes bananas when a shot, during the war, kills the officer behind him. The guilt almost drives the guy crazy ... well, I guess that's what happened to me. I did not really want the story to ever end.

Well it is going to end, but I will tell you that I feel great that I remembered as much as I did. My love of my family, my country, and my love of God carried me this far. I am looking to the future, and will continue to write. I figured it all out now. When I get through writing all the truth of my career, I will write fiction. Imagine all the fun we will have. In fiction you can make up your own beginnings, the middle, and the end to suit the readers or yourself. You can imagine to any extent. You can literally create fun, laughter, fear, just anything ...

My mother would have enjoyed this. She always said that I was going to be the lawyer in the family ... but between you and me, I always knew what she meant. She meant that I was a good talker, and a very imaginative son, whom she always loved. I am closing this last chapter in tears because of what I remembered about Mama. No wonder they had that famous play and movie, "I Remember Mama." **It is always Mama that you remember best ... Mama, this first book is for you. The next one will be for Papa ... in his own way, he was always right.** He predicted so many things that have come true.

So goodbye fans, goodbye Mama, goodbye Papa, and goodbye BOOK!

So we are at the end of the story…

Rich was seventeen months older, but I was cuter. My mother told me so, and I believed her. She was always right. I was about 4 and Rich was about 6.

Sixty years later, Rich is still 17 months older. Now you can't tell the difference!!! **I told you I would catch up to him!!!**